Disney

Paris

the mainstream
unofficial guide

Tania Alexander

MAINSTREAM
PUBLISHING

EDINBURGH AND LONDON

To Stuart, Alex and Anoushka, with all my love.

First published in Great Britain in 1995 by
MAINSTREAM PUBLISHING COMPANY (EDINBURGH) LTD
7 Albany Street
Edinburgh EH1 3UG

Reprinted 1996

ISBN 1 85158 738 1

A CIP catalogue record for this book is available from the
British Library

Typeset in ITC New Century Schoolbook by
Servis Filmsetting Ltd, Manchester
Printed and bound in Great Britain by
Caledonian International Book Manufacturing Ltd, Glasgow

Acknowledgments

I'd like to thank Celine Monget for her help with
research and translation; Sabine Marcon and
Caroline Lechaux from Disneyland Paris Press
Office for their patience and help with all my
queries; Paris Travel Service; and Stuart for all
his hard work and inspiration

*All prices quoted are as accurate as possible at
time of going to press*

Important notes

Trademarks
All characters and attractions mentioned in this book are the property of the Walt Disney Company Limited. The following names and terms included in this volume are Walt Disney registered trademarks and as such all rights to their use is courtesy of the Walt Disney Company Limited.

Adventure Isle	Fantasyland
Adventureland	Festival Disney
Audio-Animatronics	Frontierland
Discoveryland	Indiana Jones
Disneyland	Magic Kingdom
Disneyland Paris	Main Street, USA
Disneyland Paris Railroad	Walt Disney
Euro Disney	Walt Disney World

Prices
Please note that all prices are correct at time of publication. The publisher and author cannot accept responsibility for any changes which may occur.

Telephoning France
The international dialing code from the UK to France is 00 33 followed by the number (8 digits). For the city of Paris and the Greater Paris Area, dial 00 33 1 + 8 digits.

Contents

WHY 'UNOFFICIAL'?

This book is an unofficial guide to Disneyland Paris. This means that it has not been endorsed in any way by the Walt Disney Corporation, so we have been free to give an unbiased, consumer's account of everything the resort has to offer. This book has been researched by myself and a team of researchers, who have visited the park on numerous occasions, at different times of the year. On each trip we have, like you, been looking for value for money and good service.

That is not to say that this book is a negative or critical attack on Disneyland Paris. Everyone working on this book is a great Disney fan. We have been extremely impressed by this new European resort from day one and we have also noticed a lot of improvements since it first opened in April 1992.

The aim of this book is to help you make the most of your stay. So, if we have felt a restaurant or hotel is not up to scratch, we have said so. Or if any of us have been disappointed with one particular ride, this will be made quite clear. Equally, if something is an attraction not to be missed, or there is a restaurant that is well worth sampling, you will be the first to know about it.

Since the first edition of this book was published in April 1992, we have received numerous letters from readers commenting on the park and making further helpful suggestions. This was greatly appreciated, and we hope you will continue to help with future editions by sending in your personal comments and thoughts about Disneyland Paris.

Armed with this book, you should have all the unofficial and insider information necessary to make your stay truly magical and memorable.

Introduction

If you're planning a trip to Disneyland Paris, you will want to make sure that your holiday runs as smoothly as possible so that you can enjoy every minute of this magical world. This guide is for everyone who wants to get the best out of their visit to Disneyland Paris.

Whether it's just for a day or a week-long blitz, *Disneyland Paris: The Mainstream Unofficial Guide* gives you a step-by-step advice on how to plan your holiday – from booking to actually touring the resort and the surrounding area. The book tells you exactly what to expect from a holiday at Disneyland Paris, answering questions such as, what it will cost, how long are the queues, and how is the place run? Written from a travel and consumer journalist's point of view, this guidebook shows you how to get the best value out of Disneyland Paris.

Let me say right from the start that I'm as crazy about the magical world of Disney as the rest of you. As a child, I believed that elephants could fly, that if I told fibs, my nose would sprout, and that all jungle animals could calypso. I saw all the films, read the books and bought the records. My parents couldn't tear me away from the television when a Disney programme was showing.

Disney's ability both to entertain and to educate is unique. Their films are timeless, rich in detail and vivid in imagery. One minute you are watching a film, and then, suddenly, there you are in their world. Disney have an unbeatable talent to educate, inform and stimulate a youngster's imagination.

But then Disney is as much for adults as it is for children. In fact, about three-quarters of visitors to the Disney parks in the States are over 18, and Disney World has replaced Niagara Falls as America's top honeymoon destination. Whatever your age, you will love it.

Even the most hardened cynics cannot fail to be touched by the magic of their creations. When I was a child, it was too expensive to go to Disney World in the States. We had to be content with the cinema and picture-books. It was not until I was in my twenties that I made my first visit to Disney in the US. I had just left university and prided myself in being an experienced traveller. I thought I was too old and sophisticated to be going to a theme park, but as soon as I walked through those gates and strolled down Main Street, USA, my scepticism evaporated and everything I had loved about Disney as a child came flooding back. This is a fantasy land that lets us all be Peter Pan.

The Disney theme parks bring to life the stories we all know so well from the world of cinema. Instead of seeing Mickey Mouse and his friends on a screen, there they are, lifelike, before you. Instead of reading about Peter Pan, you can actually take to the skies yourself for a flight over

London and Never-Never-Land. And then there is the unique Star Tours adventure, a simulated journey into space. The first time I tried the latter I was so terrified and convinced that my plight was real that I very nearly had to pull the Emergency Stop handle! This ability to project you into their adventures is something that Disney calls 'imagineering' and no one does it better. Love it or hate it, a trip to Disney can never be an objective experience. This is interactive entertainment at its best. You are involved from the moment you walk through those gates.

The Disney parks are a world on their own and provide an escape from the unpleasant realities of life. In Disney parks there is no pollution from petrol fumes and you do not see any litter, graffiti or lager louts (alcohol is only allowed in the table-service restaurants).

Disneyland Paris, located 32 kilometres east of Paris, has opened up the magical world of Disney for thousands of Europeans. As a journalist I feel angry that some of my colleagues have painted an untrue and negative picture of Disneyland Paris. This new European park has a tremendous amount going for it and is, in many ways, superior to its American counterparts. After all, Disney belongs to Europe as much as to the States since so many of its characters are derived from classic European fairytales. The Sleeping Beauty's Castle at Disneyland Paris is by far the most beautiful of all the Disney castles and many of the attractions, such as Pirates of the Caribbean, Peter Pan's Flight, Swiss Family Robinson Tree-House and the incredible new Space Mountain, are superior in Paris.

It's the proximity of Disneyland Paris, however, that really makes it an attractive destination for Europeans. At long last, all the colour and excitement of Disney is on your doorstep. You no longer have to contend with long and tiring flights halfway across the world as you can fly to Disneyland Paris within an hour or two from the UK. Now the Channel tunnel is open, you can travel from Waterloo in London to Paris in just over three hours. Disneyland Paris is only 30 minutes from Paris by metro. Indeed, it is such an easy place to get to, that a short two-day trip or even a one-day stop-over is quite feasible.

Disneyland Paris has also been severely attacked by the European press for being far too expensive. Since it opened in April 1992 prices have been considerably reduced so that it now represents exceptionally good value – especially if you follow the guidelines and tips in this book. Also, you save money by only needing to go there for a day or two instead of spending more on a fortnight in the States.

The weather in Paris has proved a problem at Disneyland Paris. In this new edition of the book we have included a whole chapter (see page 199) on coping with the rain so that you will know all the best places to go if there is a downpour.

Disney is renowned for its superb organisation and management skills. But even in their world, you will find that you still have to queue for the most popular attractions. There's no magic formula, even here! That's where this guide can help. We have carefully planned a selection of Unofficial Guided Tours to help you avoid the worst of the queues and see the best of the attractions. We have devised tours both for adults, and families with young children. Only got one day? Fine. Follow our Whirlwind Tours and you'll find you can pack in all the best rides with time for lunch in between.

Of course, we do recommend you spend more time in exploring the wonders of Disney, so if you've got two days, enjoy our special Two-Day Tours and sample all the attractions with plenty of time to try out your favourites again.

If you're lucky enough to be spending a week or more at Disneyland Paris, you'll find a complete guide to all that the site has to offer, as well as the many attractions of the surrounding countryside. We have included a special chapter on excursions beyond Disneyland Paris, detailing all sorts of day trips accessible from the theme park. Why not visit a local vineyard (the Champagne region is only a short drive away), spend a day in the old city of Chantilly or enjoy the white-knuckle rides at the local French theme park, Parc Asterix? We've included details of all sorts of local sporting fac- ilities, from windsurfing on a nearby lake to horseriding in the forests of Fontainebleau. Or why not take a trip to the magical capital of Paris – it's only a half-hour train ride away so we have included details of all the highlights that you may want to see in a day's excursion.

Most people who go to Disneyland Paris are travelling with young children and this in itself can turn any trip into a survival guide. In this new edition of the book we have included a special chapter entitled 'Taking Young Children to Disneyland Paris' (see page 191) so that it all goes as smoothly as possible for you and your kids.

All the rides and attractions at Disneyland

Paris have been graded (* to *****) so that you can tell at a glance whether any particular one is worth while. Similarly, we have reviewed and graded all the table-service restaurants, shops and entertainment facilities.

As accommodation is such an important part of any holiday, we have carefully reviewed all the hotels on site, as well as finding other places in the area for you to stay, ranging from cheap bed and breakfasts to luxury châteaux.

Throughout the book, we have put an emphasis on getting value for money so that you will find many ways to cut the cost of your holiday, from booking cheaper accommodation to eating at the more reasonably priced restaurants.

We've also included details of the best route to take if you are driving, places to stop for food and refreshments on the way down, and a special Disney Quiz to entertain all the family. Finally, in Chapter Fifteen, we tell you where to find your children's favourite characters in the park.

Whether this is your first visit to Disney or your fifth, I hope this book will tell you everything you need to know and help to make your stay a truly magical experience.

CHAPTER ONE

WHAT TO EXPECT FROM A HOLIDAY AT DISNEYLAND PARIS

This chapter gives you some background information to Disneyland Paris and answers the sort of questions you may ask before booking a holiday.

APRIL 1992: MICKEY ARRIVED IN EUROPE!

Disney are veterans in the field of theme parks. When the first Disney resort, Disneyland, opened in California in 1955, Walt Disney called it 'the happiest place on earth'. Today, he would have to refer to it as 'one of' the happiest places on earth as there are now four Disney pleasure parks, spread over three continents. Mickey Mouse is set to rule the world.

Walt Disney World opened in Florida in 1971 and Tokyo Disneyland began operating in 1983. Euro Disneyland (as it was first called) opened just outside Paris in 1992 and is the fourth and latest Disney resort. Based on the original Magic Kingdom at Disneyland in California, the European park has also been influenced by the Florida and Tokyo parks.

A CENTRAL LOCATION

Disneyland Paris is located 32 km east of Paris in the Marne-la Vallée on what was originally a 5,000-acre site of flat beet fields. It is an ideal location for a European Disney resort as it is located along the A4 expressway that runs from Paris to Strasbourg and is, therefore, easily accessible from most central European countries.

Although you never really feel as though you are in France when you are inside the theme park, the atmosphere is very cosmopolitan with tourists from all over Europe.

HEIGH-HO, HEIGH-HO, IT'S OFF TO WORK WE GO . . .

The construction of Euro Disney began in earnest in August 1988 and involved the removal of more than four million cubic metres of earth and the planting of hundreds of thousands of trees.

Disneyland Paris employs 10,000 workers, the majority of whom are French, although Disney has recruited staff from all over Europe including the UK. Disney employees are called 'cast members' who star in the park's attractions, shops and restaurants, offer Disney smiles and hospitality to guests in the resort hotels, or work backstage providing administrative support.

The Euro Disney Casting Centre opened on 1 September 1991. Disney was clearly looking for a certain type of employee. 'The main qualities necessary for all cast members are friendliness, warmth and a genuine interest in people,' they said.

Cast members have to be bilingual (French and English) and prepared to follow strict, disciplinarian rules. Female cast have to wear 'appropriate underwear' – fishnet stockings and suspenders are out. So are earrings larger than a penny piece, obviously dyed hair, mini-skirts and make-up that does not look natural. They are also not allowed to wear more than one ring on each hand. The male cast are not allowed visible tattoos, long hair, beards or moustaches. Both sexes are required to wear deodorant and are forbidden to be overweight.

WILL THEY SPEAK ENGLISH?

All the cast members in the park are supposed to speak English. In the many times we've visited, we

17

have only come across one or two cast members who couldn't speak English, and there was always another cast member near at hand to offer interpretation. You can tell at a glance what languages cast members speak by the badges of national flags which are prominently displayed on their jackets.

A BEAUTIFUL WORLD

The minute you walk through the turnstiles at Disneyland Paris you enter a beautiful world without litter or graffiti. Everything is kept spotlessly clean, from the roads in the park to the floors in the restaurants. There are thousands of litter boxes strategically placed – so there is no excuse for dropping anything on the perfectly swept streets. Litter attendants are dressed in white and seem to pick up cigarette ends and stray pieces of litter before they even reach the ground! Benches are kept clean and are immediately towelled down after a downpour.

THE WEATHER

Disneyland Paris is open 365 days a year. Unless you go in the height of the summer, you should be prepared for cool, wet weather (see Chapter Eleven entitled Coping with the Rain). There is nothing worse than sitting shivering on the rides or queuing in the rain with no protection. Even though Disneyland Paris has more covered areas than the parks in the States, you can still get very cold and wet there since some exposure to the elements is inevitable. Make sure you pack some warm, waterproof clothing.

MORE THAN A THEME PARK . . .

Disneyland Paris has been created as a giant pleasure resort – a place you would go to for a holiday
rather than a day trip. Unlike other local theme
parks such as Parc Asterix (see page 243),
Disneyland Paris has on-site hotels which are
attractions in themselves. Each provide health
clubs, shops and restaurants and are based on
themes inspired by a particular American time or
place. Once you are in the resort, there is no need
to step outside, as everything from banking services to swimming-pools, golf and tennis facilities
is on-site.

WILL THE CHILDREN COPE WITH
THE RIDES?

Children of all ages will enjoy Disneyland Paris.
Little children and toddlers will probably appreciate the characters more than the rides although
some small children may find a giant-sized Mickey
Mouse a little daunting. Some rides such as Star
Tours and Space Mountain have height restrictions and are more suited to older children. See
Chapter Ten for more information and advice
about taking young children to Disneyland Paris.

WHAT WILL THE QUEUES BE LIKE?

There are always queues for the most popular
attractions such as Big Thunder Mountain and
Space Mountain. This book, however, will help you
avoid the worst queues and enable you to spend
more time on the rides. Chapter Twelve outlines

detailed tours to help you minimise the time spent queueing.

FACILITIES FOR DISABLED PEOPLE

Disneyland Paris has been designed with disabled people in mind. All the hotels have special rooms and most of the restaurants have special toilets. People with wheelchairs are given priority on all the rides. Disney's *Guest Special Services Guide* (available from the Main Entrance and from City Hall in Main Street, USA) outlines special access to attractions, restaurants and shops. Wheelchairs can be hired in Main Street, USA.

Sight-impaired visitors may make use of the complimentary audio cassettes and portable tape players which are provided at City Hall, and guide dogs are allowed in most of the park. Complimentary use of a special telephone device is also provided at City Hall for hearing-impaired visitors.

HOW DOES DISNEYLAND PARIS DIFFER FROM THE AMERICAN PARKS?

Although Disneyland Paris is based on the original Disneyland's Magic Kingdom, there are aspects about this new park that are distinctly European. Sleeping Beauty's castle has become the Château de la Belle au Bois Dormant and most people think it is the most beautiful of all the Disney castles, perhaps influenced by the French art of building châteaux. The futuristic theme land, Discoveryland, is unique to Disneyland Paris and is inspired by the work of European artists and writers such as Leonardo da Vinci, H.G. Wells and Jules Verne. Space Mountain (opens in June 1995) is one of the most exciting and thrilling of all the Disney attractions on both sides of the Atlantic.

Disneyland Paris is also smaller than the American parks. It covers 5,000 acres (one-fifth of the size of Paris) compared to the 28,000 acres of Disney World – which is twice the size of Manhattan. In keeping with European standards, the hotel rooms are also smaller at Disneyland Paris.

The menus and food pricing at Disneyland Paris have changed dramatically since it first opened. The park is now full of fast-food restaurants serving hot dogs, burgers, chips and pizzas at a similar price to those in Paris (see Chapter Seven for further details about eating out).

HOW LONG SHOULD I GO FOR?

As you will see from our Whirlwind Tour (see page 205) it is perfectly possible to see the best of Disneyland Paris in one day. However, if you are travelling with young children or you want to enjoy the park at more leisure, you really need two or three days.

WHAT SHOULD I PACK?

Your most important item is a comfortable pair of trainers or walking shoes, as you will be on your feet for much of the day. Anoraks, hats and waterproof clothing are a must in winter; indeed, it is best to be prepared for wet, chilly weather for most of the year – apart from summer. Money belts are a much safer option than handbags. And don't forget your camera, plenty of film and a pencil so you can do the quiz in Chapter Fifteen!

DISNEYSPEAK

Finally, when you go to Disneyland Paris, you will soon notice that this magical land has a language all of its own. Here are some special Disney words and their meanings:

Adult – anyone over the age of 12 is an adult and pays the full entrance fee.

Cabins – mobile homes in Camp Davy Crockett.

Cast members – Disney employees.

Disney spirit – big smiles and the cast's ability to never look flustered.

Disney University – training centre for cast.

Greeter – attendant welcoming you on to a ride.

Guests – paying visitors to Disney.

Guest relations – information desk.

Guest rooms – hotel rooms.

Members of the Disney Participant Family – sponsors.

Retail Entertainment Centres – shops.

Pre-Entertainment Area – queues.

CHAPTER TWO

WHAT WILL IT COST?

So, you've decided that you want to go to Disneyland Paris, but are not exactly sure what it is going to cost. This chapter details everything you are likely to have to pay for during a holiday in Disneyland Paris, from the initial travel package to extras such as drinks and snacks. By following our guidelines you'll be able to get better value for money and be able to budget more accurately before you even set off.

Incidentally, prices at Disneyland Paris have been considerably reduced since 1992 so that you now pay less for entrance tickets, hotel accommodation, food and shopping.

WILL IT COST MORE THAN A HOLIDAY IN THE STATES?

Despite the new pricings, Disneyland Paris is still slightly dearer than the parks in the States. This discrepancy is mainly due to the exchange rate. But, since you'll probably only stay for a couple of days, it need not put you out of pocket – particularly if you follow the guidelines in this book.

If you are on a tight budget, the cheapest way to go to Disneyland Paris is to stay in a local campsite, motel or auberge (see page 58 for suggested places). You can find a room in a local motel for under 150F per night. There are also tour operators who sell packages using cheap, off-site accommodation (see page 34), but check to make sure they include guaranteed entry to the theme park – otherwise you will have to pay 150F per day in entrance fees.

The Disney accommodation is superb both in quality and atmosphere, and hotel room prices start at 300F per night. The top hotel is Hotel Disneyland which is located right at the entrance to the park, overlooking Main Street, USA. Prices in this hotel start at 1,650F per night.

Another alternative is to stay in Paris itself and commute to Disneyland Paris on the RER metro network. (The journey from Paris to Disneyland takes 30 minutes.)

If you are looking for luxury accommodation outside Disney there are several beautiful châteaux in the nearby countryside. A room in a château will cost you from about 450F per night.

See Chapter Four, giving full details of where to stay and for reviews of hotels.

A VALUE-FOR-MONEY DAY

Entrance tickets to the park cost from 150F per adult with reductions for children (see page 35 for full details). This ticket represents excellent value for money as it includes entrance to all the rides and attractions, plus it gives you the opportunity to watch the superb parades and shows. In the summer, make the most of your ticket by staying in the park and enjoying your favourite rides again in the dark.

THE MORE THE MERRIER!

It is more economical to travel as a family or group of four than as a couple or a single person because all the Disneyland Paris accommodation, and most of the off-site accommodation, charge for the room regardless of how many people occupy it. For example, a family of four can stay at Hotel Santa Fe for 300F per night (which works out at 75F per person). Bear in mind, however, that rooms in the budget Disney hotels are very compact so that to have four in there will be quite a crush!

If you are travelling on your own, it should be cheaper to stay outside the resort.

SHOULD I BOOK INDEPENDENTLY OR AS PART OF A PACKAGE?

It usually works out cheaper to buy a package which includes an entrance pass. Both Disney and selected tour operators now sell packages that include accommodation and entrance to the park. (See Chapter Three for full details about booking your holiday.)

HOW MUCH WILL A PACKAGE COST?

A typical cheap package costs from £71 per person for two nights at the Santa Fe with Paris Travel Service. This is based on a family of two adults and two children sharing a room, and includes ferry crossing, accommodation, breakfast and guaranteed free entry to the park for the length of your stay. The same packages cost £143 per person flying from Heathrow. (See page 33 for further details of tour operators.)

WHAT WILL IT COST ME TO GET THERE?

The cheapest ways to get to Disneyland Paris are by coach or self-drive (with four people in the car) – obviously, this depends on which part of the UK you are travelling from. If you are staying on site, you will not need a car but self-drive is ideal if you plan to extend your stay by touring the area.

HOW MUCH WILL THE PETROL AND TOLLS COST?

Depending on your make of car you should be able to drive to Disneyland Paris (less than 200 miles from Calais) on a full tank of petrol. Petrol costs slightly more in France than in the UK, although diesel is considerably cheaper.

The quickest way to get there is on the autoroutes. Toll charges are 81F from Calais to Disneyland Paris and 94F from Disneyland Paris to Calais.

CAR HIRE

If you want to explore the local countryside (see Chapter Thirteen, entitled Excursions) you can hire a car. The official firm at Disneyland Paris is Europcar. A day's car hire costs 580F.

HOW MUCH SPENDING MONEY SHOULD I TAKE?

Most package holidays now include breakfast, and a few also include half-board. If you are on a bed-and-breakfast package, a daily budget of 250–350F per person would not be extravagant, allowing you to eat out twice a day and do a little shopping.

EATING OUT

This will be your most expensive outlay, particularly if you are staying in the resort. The restaurants in the park are all similarly priced – 30–50F for a set meal comprising main course, drink and dessert in a fast-food restaurant (25–32F children), and 140F for a three-course set menu in a table-service restaurant (45F children). (See Chapter Seven for full details of eating out and recommended restaurants.)

To give you an idea of the cost of living at Disneyland Paris, following is a list of some of the items that you may want to buy in the park.

burger (small) 8F
chips 10–15F
sandwich 18F
hot dog (small) 13F

ice-cream 9F
coffee 6F
coke (50cl) 12F
mineral water (50cl) 10F
pizza (small) 18F

CUTTING THE COST OF YOUR HOLIDAY

- There are many food carts offering reasonably priced snacks for lunch or dinner (for example 13F for a hot dog). Or fill up French-style on a bag of frites (10F) at Café Brousse in Adventureland.
- If you're starving hungry, opt for set menus, such as the 50F Mickey meal which comprises a main course, drink and dessert in a fast-food restaurant, or the 140F menus in the table-service restaurants.
- Book a half-board package if you intend to eat in your hotel in the evening.
- Go in the middle of the week rather than at weekends when package prices are cheaper and the crowds disappear.
- Look out for special deals and promotions such as Kids Free at certain times of the year.
- Pack a warm jumper and waterproofs and go in the winter when hotel and entrance ticket prices are lower.

CHAPTER THREE

BOOKING YOUR HOLIDAY

This chapter tells you how to get to Disneyland Paris and the best ways to book your holiday.

Disneyland Paris and Resort Complex

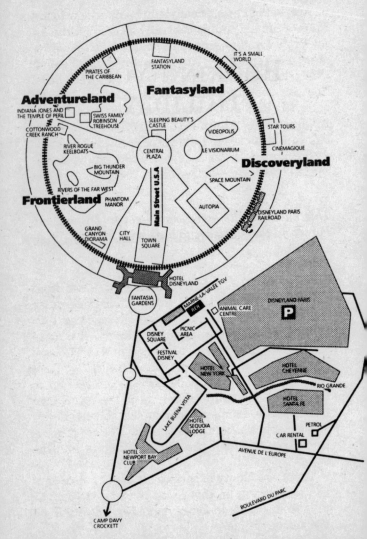

DISNEYLAND PARIS

HOW TO GET THERE

32 km east of Paris, Disneyland Paris is easy to get to from the UK and is centrally located on the A4 for France and nearby European countries. Eurostar now enables you to travel from London (Waterloo) to Paris (Gare du Nord) in three hours. You can then cross over to Châtelet in Paris to catch the RER metro which takes you to the resort in 35 minutes. Alternatively, the TGV high-speed rail runs direct from Lille to the resort in one hour. Disneyland Paris is also near two international airports – Charles de Gaulle and Orly.

BY CAR

Journey time: Approximately three and a half hours from Calais.

Disneyland Paris is approximately 328 km from Calais, an easy but dull drive along autoroutes and main roads. From Calais, follow the A26 through St Omer towards Arras. From Arras, take the A1 towards Paris, turning off after Roissy-Charles de Gaulle Airport on to the A104. Then take the N2 towards Soissons and turn off on to the A104. This will lead you on to the A4. Follow the A4 in the Reims direction and you will shortly see an abundance of Disneyland Paris signposts on your left. Follow these signs directly into the resort.

There are plenty of service stations and restaurants to stop at on this route. It costs 81F for the tolls from Calais to Disneyland Paris and 95F on the journey home.

AA Roadwatch has a Disney information line (Tel: 0836 401400) giving details of routes from the Channel ports, traffic hold-ups and a weather report.

Parking: Disneyland Paris has a huge carpark with space for 11,000 cars. It costs 40F per day. Don't forget to make a note of the exact area (named after Disney characters such as Bambi, Tigger and Pinocchio) where you park or you will have to wait until thousands of cars have exited before you find yours! A moving walkway transports you to the park entrance. Disabled visitors can park next to the Disneyland Hotel. Hotel guests use the hotel carparks.

BY TRAIN

Journey time: Approximately three hours by Eurostar from Waterloo station to Paris Gare du Nord. You then have to cross over to Châtelet to take the RER metro (35 minutes) direct to the resort. Alternatively, you can travel by Eurostar to Lille (approximately 90 minutes) and then change on to the TGV high-speed train which takes a further hour to arrive at Disneyland Paris.

For further details and bookings telephone Eurostar 0233 617575

BY PLANE

Journey time: Approximately one hour by plane from London Heathrow to Roissy-Charles de Gaulle or Orly, then 30–60 minutes transfer depending on traffic. There are shuttle buses from both airports to Disneyland Paris or you can catch the TGV from Roissy-Charles de Gaulle to the resort (15 minutes).

BY COACH

Journey time: Approximately four and a half hours from Calais to Disneyland Paris by coach.
Several tour operators run package holidays with coach transport to Disneyland Paris (or to accommodation in Paris). See below.

WHEN TO GO THERE

Disneyland Paris is open 365 days a year. In order to avoid the worst of the crowds, it is best not to book during the French school holidays, Easter, 1 May (Labour Day in France, Belgium and Germany) or Bastille Day (14 July). If you are planning a short trip, mid-week is also quieter (and packages then are usually cheaper) than weekends.

MAKING YOUR RESERVATION

Holiday packages and room reservations can be booked direct with Disney by telephoning 0733 33 5505 in the UK, (407) W-DISNEY in the USA or (33 1) 60 30 60 30 in France. Information and bookings are also available from most travel agents.

TOUR OPERATORS

The following tour operators sell package holidays to Disney:

Air France
(Tel: 0181 742 3377)
Packages to all Disney hotels and Camp Davy Crockett with departures from a large selection of UK airports. Breakfast and entrance tickets included in the packages.

P & O European Ferries
(Tel: 01992 456045)
Packages to all Disney hotels and Camp Davy Crockett. Includes breakfast and entrance tickets. Half-board packages available.

Paris Travel Service
(Tel: 0992 456100)
All Disney hotels and Camp Davy Crockett. Also accommodation in Paris. Choice of travel by air, self-drive or Eurostar. Includes breakfast and entrance tickets. Also 'Character Teas' (unique to Paris Travel Service) and half-board option.

Cresta Holidays
(Tel: 0161 9269999)
All Disney hotels and Camp Davy Crockett. Also hotels in surrounding area or in Paris. Choice of travel by air, self-drive or Eurostar via Lille. Accommodation includes breakfast and entrance tickets.

Abbey Travel
(Tel: 010 35318 724 188)
All Disney hotels and Camp Davy Crockett; room only. Includes travel by air and entrance tickets. Also accommodation in Paris.

Cosmos Coach Tours
(Tel: 0161 4805799)
Disney hotels and Camp Davy Crockett. Room
only basis, includes entrance tickets. Travel by
coach from all over UK. Also Supersaver holidays
staying in Paris and busing in to Disneyland Paris
each day. Travel by air is also available.

ASSURED ENTRY

There are many other tour operators who can
include entrance tickets to Disneyland Paris in a
package. These tour operators offer off-site accommodation in nearby hotels or in Paris. Do check
when booking that the tour operator you choose
can guarantee you access to the resort.

TRAVELLING INDEPENDENTLY

One of the cheapest ways to go to Disneyland Paris
is to book your own off-site accommodation (see
page 52 for places to stay). One, two or three-day
passports can be bought at the main gate of
Disneyland Paris.

ADMISSION CHARGES

Charges vary according to season:
One day: 150–195F (120–150F children under 12).
Two days: 285–370F (230–285F children under 12)
Three days: 390–505F (310–390F children under
12)
Free entrance for children under three.
The entrance fee allows you free unlimited use of
all rides and attractions, except the Rustler

Roundup Shootin' Gallery. The park's opening hours vary according to season so check when booking. In summer months it stays open until late at night.

Annual entrance tickets are also available. The Annual Passport, costing 695F (495F for children under 12 years old), gives free entry to the park for a year, except on certain weekends and public holidays. It also entitles you to buy a one-year parking-pass for 140F. An Annual Passport Plus costs 995F (695F for children under 12 years old) and includes free entry to the park for a year without any date restrictions, plus free parking for a year. It also includes discounts in restaurants and shops.

CHAPTER FOUR

WHERE TO STAY

*There are three main choices of accommodation.
You can either stay on-site in Disney's hotels, nearby in local accommodation, or in Paris itself.*

*In this chapter we review Disney's hotels and
also suggest some other local places to stay.*

ACCOMMODATION IN DISNEYLAND PARIS

There are six Disney hotels and a campsite, designed by American and French architects. Each hotel is a themed attraction in itself, so staying there continues the Disney holiday experience.

One of the advantages of the Disney hotels is that they are all located close to the theme park so there is no commuting and all the restaurants and entertainment are on your doorstep. If you are staying in Disney's accommodation you do not need your own car as you can walk everywhere or use their free shuttle bus service.

The Disneyland Hotel is the only hotel on the doorstep of the park. The other hotels are within 20 minutes leisurely walk of the park. They also have a shuttle bus service which is easy to use as it runs so frequently. The drawback in bad weather is that the bus drops you off about 5–10 minutes walk from the park which rather defeats the purpose of taking the bus in the first place as you are going to get soaked anyway (see Chapter Eleven: Coping with the Rain).

Prices in the Disney hotels have been considerably reduced since they first opened although they still cost more than local hotels nearby. However, with Disney you are guaranteed good quality, excellent facilities and polite service. The rooms are all designed to sleep four, most with two double beds, so they do work out more economical for families than for couples or single people. Be prepared, however, for smaller rooms than in the States and for baths that have been designed with very short people in mind! There are interconnecting rooms for families and suites for those requiring more space. Non-smoking and rooms for disabled people are also available.

One niggle about the Disney hotels is that you cannot book in until 3 p.m., sometimes later if your room is not ready. The cast members are trained to apologise, smile sweetly and to suggest that you leave your luggage with them and go straight off to the theme park. If you have driven all the way from the UK, this is probably the last thing you feel like doing, particularly if you have weary children in tow. From personal experience, we suggest that you have a leisurely drive down to Disneyland Paris, stop for lunch on the way, and don't try to book in until after 3 p.m.

All the Disney hotels are huge, so checking in and out can be quite a tedious process. Eating in the hotel restaurants can also be problematic as some of them (such as the ones at Sequoia Lodge) do not have a big enough seating capacity so queues are quick to build up. It's best to stagger your meal times – either eating before the 7.30 p.m. crush or after 9 p.m.

There are six hotels of different price categories, all based on a theme of a particular American region and period, as well as a campground called Camp Davy Crockett. These are all reviewed below.

CONVENTION TIME

The bigger hotels, such as Hotel New York and Sequoia Lodge, are popular venues for business conventions. Staying at one of these hotels with young children during a convention is not ideal – be prepared for noisy business people to bang on your door at 3 a.m! The Cheyenne and the Santa

Fe are excellent value hotels for families and have the added bonus of not catering for conventions.

CREDIT CARDS

All the hotels accept American Express, Eurocard, Master Card, Visa, Carte Bleue, travellers' checks and Eurocheques.

Currencies can be exchanged at all the receptions.

The prices quoted below are for the room rate only, when booked directly with Disneyland Paris (Tel: 0733 33 5505).

THE DISNEYLAND HOTEL

Price of rooms: From 1,650 to 1,990F per room, per night.

Overall opinion

The best location of all the Disney hotels and very pretty.

Description

This is the top Disneyland Paris hotel, styled like a candy-pink Victorian palace with a giant Mickey Mouse clockface and twinkling lights outside. The inside is decorated with pretty pastel colours, Disney paintings and daintily carved Tinkerbells on the furniture.

Apart from being so pretty, the main attraction of this luxury hotel is its location – right at the entrance to the theme park, overlooking Main Street, USA and the Magic Kingdom.

The hotel, which will appeal to little girls with rich daddies, was obviously not to the liking of Don

Johnson and Melanie Griffith, who apparently booked out and transferred to the stark, yet more sophisticated Hotel New York when they came over for the park opening in April 1992. However, because of its location and impressive style, this will always be a popular hotel and it is already fully booked for New Year's Eve 1999!

Children's Rating

Children will love this hotel as the decor is so pretty and they are staying so near the park and their favourite characters. It is good for parents with young children as it's easy to take them back at lunchtime for a nap.

Guest Rooms

There are 500 rooms, including 21 suites, the best of which overlook the theme park. In keeping with the rest of the hotel, the rooms are decorated in pretty, pastel colours with light, wood furniture and Tinkerbell carvings on the wardrobes. The suites are named after Disney characters such as Bambi.

Facilities

Disneyland Pool and Club offers a gym, jacuzzi, sauna, solarium, steam-room, indoor swimming-pool and a games room. There are aerobics and massage facilities and an in-room baby-sitting service.

Eating and Drinking

Main Street Lounge: Elegant place to sit and sip a cocktail, overlooking Main Street, USA.
Café Fantasia: A fun Disney-themed café where the family can meet for a big ice-cream sundae at the end of the day.

Inventions: Buffet meals of regional American cuisine, for breakfast, lunch and dinner.
California Grill: Casual, elegant dining with Californian cuisine.

Shopping

Galerie Mickey: Victorian-style shop selling usual Disney memorabilia, cuddly toys, etc, as well as designer clothes.

HOTEL NEW YORK

Price of rooms: 1,025F per night.

Overall opinion

Stylish hotel with ice rink outside in winter and superb jazz club. More suited for uptown couples and individuals than families.

Description

This luxury hotel looks like a comic book cut-out, a pastiche of New York architecture, complete with Manhattan Tower, Gramercy Park Wing, Brownstone buildings and a Rockefeller Centre outdoor ice-skating rink.

The overall effect is stark and the cold, business-like atmosphere is enhanced by the adjoining New York Coliseum Convention Centre. The rust and grey interior colour scheme represents the drabber characteristics of Art Deco. There are, however, some nice design details such as the stylist Art Deco elevators.

The outdoor ice-rink is also a hive of activity in the winter. A two-hour session will cost 50F (40F for children).

Children's Rating
Not much fun, except in winter when the outdoor ice-skating rink is open.

Guest Rooms
575 Art Deco-themed rooms, including 36 suites. A typical room has stripy wallpaper, a Big Apple drinks cabinet (housing TV and mini bar), a table light in the shape of the Empire State Building and New York pictures. There are no balconies in this hotel.

Facilities
Two floodlit tennis courts. Outdoor ice-skating rink (in winter only). Hairdressers/beauty salon. Games arcade. Downtown Athletic Club featuring aerobics and gym, jacuzzi, massage, sauna, solarium, steam-room and an ugly-looking swimming-pool, the indoor section of which looks as though it is housed in an industrial building. In-room baby-sitting service is also available.

Eating and Drinking
Club Manhattan: Elegant bar with superb live jazz.
57th Street Bar: Laid-back place for a drink in the lobby of the hotel. Log fires make this one of the cosier areas in the hotel.
Parkside Diner: New York-style diner – good for breakfast.

Shopping
Stock Exchange: Disney memorabilia (cuddly toys, etc) as well as New York souvenirs such as t-shirts and hold-alls (fun for teenagers) and designer clothes.

NEWPORT BAY CLUB

Price of rooms: From 625 to 875F per room per night.

Overall opinion
Most elegant of all the hotels and the nautical theme works well. Recommended.

Description
This is a very attractive hotel at the far side of Lake Buena Vista, built in the style of an elegant New England turn-of-the-century beach palace.

The nautical theme works very well with port-holes in the corridor doors, cast members dressed like sailors and a giant globe in the lobby which fascinates the kids. The decor (predominantly navy, red and white) is simplistic but stylish and the yacht-club atmosphere is enhanced by a harbour lighthouse and a veranda with rocking chairs overlooking the lake.

Children's Rating
Great fun, particularly for teenagers.

Guest Rooms
This is a huge hotel with 1,098 rooms, including 15 suites. The best rooms overlook the lake. All the rooms have a nautical theme with schooner-printed curtains, nautical bed heads, bold stripy wallpaper in the bathrooms, and a bright design that would delight most teenage boys.

Facilities
The Nantucket indoor-outdoor swimming-pool is particularly attractive. The health club also

offers aerobics and gym, jacuzzi, massage, sauna, solarium and steam-room. There is a croquet field, games arcade and children's playground with look-out tower. In-room baby-sitting service is provided.

Eating and Drinking
Fisherman's Wharf: Comfortable lounge bar off the main lobby, overlooking the lake. Cosmopolitan atmosphere with live piano music every night.
Cape Cod: Informal restaurant with an American menu of pizzas, fresh seafood and pastas.
Yacht Club: A more formal restaurant serving speciality shellfish. (Both restaurants were enlarged in 1995.)

Shopping
Bay Boutique: Standard Disney memorabilia. Also Osh Kosh children's wear and clothing with a nautical theme.

SEQUOIA LODGE

Price of rooms: From 525 to 775F

Overall opinion
The least Disneyfied hotel. Huge rustic retreat, devoid of much character or theming. Best bar.

Description
You can smell the pine needles as you walk round the beautiful wooded grounds of this hotel, which has been built in the style of a lodge in the American National Parks.

45

The inside of the hotel is rather a disappointment. The downstairs bar with its huge fire is indeed splendid but the rest of the hotel is dull and sprawling with dowdy looking bedrooms and a particularly boring family restaurant called Beaver Creek.

In winter there is a tiny, indoor play area in the lounge with a tatty bit of carpet, a sadly depleted supply of Lego, a rocking horse and a TV showing surprisingly poor quality Disney videos. Families would do much better staying at the Cheyenne which is also cheaper.

Children's Rating
More of a peaceful retreat for the grown-ups.

Guest Rooms
There are 1,011 hunting lodge-style rooms, including 14 suites. The bedrooms are rather oppressive with little space as they have two small double beds or one large, king-size bed in them. They are decorated with redwood furnishings, patchwork-quilt duvets and pictures of wildlife or mountain scenes. Bathrooms are small and uninspiring with the sink outside the bathroom opposite the wardrobe space.

Facilities
Quarry Pool Health Club offers aerobics, gym, jacuzzi, massage, sauna, solarium, steam-room and attractive indoor-outdoor swimming-pool. The pool area is in a building in the hotel grounds so you have to go outside to get there which is not ideal on a cold, wet day. Game arcade room. Children's playground. In-room baby-sitting service.

Eating and Drinking

Redwood Bar and Lounge: Large atmospheric bar with a huge log fire and live piano music. Best of all the Disney hotel bars.

Beaver Creek Tavern: Serves standard family fare such as burgers and pasta. Uninspiring.

Hunter's Grill: Rôtisserie specialising in marinated meats.

Shopping

Northwest Passage: Disney memorabilia and national park theme gifts.

HOTEL CHEYENNE

Price of rooms: From 400 to 675F per room, per night.

Overall opinion

The most imaginative of all the Disney hotels. Great fun and good value for families. Best family restaurant.

Description

This hotel is styled like a frontier town of the American West. You feel as though you are staying on a film set and that John Wayne is going to come busting out of one of the guest buildings at any moment!

The Wild West atmosphere starts from the moment you arrive when the cast members welcome you with a loud 'Howdy!'

There is a big log fire in the large bustling reception area. Rooms are located in themed frontier guest buildings along Main Street. Children will

love it here as it is an ideal setting for playing cowboys and Indians amongst covered wagons, wig-
wams and teepees. In summer there are pony
rides and barbeques on the square.

Children's Rating

Brilliant fun. They won't want to stay anywhere
else!

Guest Rooms

There are 1,000 rooms. The rooms are small but
have been designed with much imagination. There
are holes from gun shots in the wooden double bed
and there are bunk beds for the children. Other
details include a wooden mini bar with lone star
motif, a lamp in the shape of a cowboy boot and
curtains made out of what looks like a giant cowboy's scarf. There is even buffalo-printed carpet!
Two-thirds of the rooms are interconnecting.

Facilities

Fort Apache playground and Indian Village for the
children. Arcade games room. In-room baby-sitting service.

Eating and Drinking

Red Garter Saloon: Cosy Wild West saloon bar
with log fire and live country music in the
evenings.
Chuck Wagon Café: Best hotel restaurant for families. Large self-service restaurant with pioneer-
style dishes which you select from specialist
wagons such as the Range Rider Barbeque Pit,
Cowgirls' Salad Wagon and the Last Chance
Watering Hole. Lots of space for lively kids to run

about with leather saddle seats at the bar and a large wooden horse and truck in the middle of the dining room for them to climb on. Breakfast is superb with steaming porridge served out of cowboy bowls, giant plates of berries and fresh fruit, pancakes with maple syrup and other cooked dishes. Also good for dinner with huge plates of barbequed food.

Shopping
General Store: Disney memorabilia and western theme goods.

HOTEL SANTA FE

Price of rooms: From 300 to 550F per room, per night.

Overall opinion
Good value for families but rather cheap and tacky looking.

Description
Styled on the American South-west, this is the least inspiring of all the Disney accommodation with barren-looking New Mexico desert surrounds, dusty-looking buildings and a billboard poster of Clint Eastwood at the entrance.

The reception area is characterless and uninviting. It is the sort of hotel you would expect to find on a cheap package holiday to the Canary Islands.

Children's Rating
They will prefer to stay at the Cheyenne on the other side of the Rio Grande river.

Guest Rooms
There are 1,000 Santa Fe-style rooms in 42 pueblos.
The decor in the room is bright and cheerful with
Aztec-style patchwork bedspreads.

Facilities
Totem Circle Playground. Pow Wow game arcade
room. In-room baby-sitting service.

Eating and Drinking
Rio Grande Bar: Serving cocktails such as Jose's
Pick Up, Tequila Sunrise, Howling Coyote and
Sombrero. Live music in the evenings.
La Cantina: Friendly self-service-style restaurant
offering a variety of American Tex-Mex speciali-
ties, such as black bean soup and chilli con carne.

Shopping
Trading Post: Small shop selling Disney memorabilia and New Mexico theme goods.

DAVY CROCKETT RANCH

Price of cabins: From 1,090 to 2,350F for four
nights during the week. 1,390–2,350F for three-
night weekends, 2,110–3,995F for a week.

Overall opinion
Great fun for families in a relaxing, wooded location.

Description
When you drive in under the entrance and see
Mickey Mouse dressed up as Davy Crockett on the
name plate, you'll realise that this is no ordinary
campsite.

Situated about six miles away from Disneyland Paris, children will love this wooded campsite, which is designed in early American pioneer style with a western fort and log cabins. The latter are actually just mobile homes decked in wood, but they are extremely spacious and luxurious, each with a dishwasher, microwave, colour TV, telephone, outdoor picnic table and barbeque. There is one bedroom with double bed and bunk beds and another pull-out double bed in the lounge. Bathrooms are small but the baths themselves are actually bigger than in some of the Disney hotels.

One of the main financial advantages of staying in this campsite is that you can self-cater. The village store stocks food although it is more economical to come with a well-stocked car or drive out to a local supermarket for provisions.

The log cabins are grouped in trails in fairly close proximity – with everyone's car parked outside their home, it actually looks very suburban. You wake up in the morning, however, to the sound of the bird's singing and the overall atmosphere is very relaxing.

Apart from the 414 cabins, there are also 181 campsites, each with water, washing facilities, electrical hook-ups and a picnic table.

It is a shame that the village (where you will find Crockett's Tavern, Davy's Farm, Blue Springs Pool and tennis courts) is located so close to the motorway as the roar of passing vehicles spoils the illusion of a wilderness retreat.

Children's Rating
They'll love it! The superb facilities for children (see below) mean that you could easily spend a

couple of days in the camp without venturing out to Disneyland Paris.

Facilities
Davy's Farm gives little children a chance to stroke their favourite farmyard animals and go on pony rides. Bicycle rentals provide a healthy way to travel round the camp. Nature, bike and jogging trails. Sports fields, tennis courts, campfire, children's playgrounds.

Blue Springs Pool is a stunning indoor swimming complex next to the restaurant with slides, river waterfall, spa and health-food bar. Modest swimmers may feel self-conscious that the changing-rooms are communal although you can change in your own cubicle! Our only criticism was that it is not very hygienic since you can walk through the changing-rooms to the pool in outdoor shoes.

Eating and Drinking
Crockett's Tavern: Small, bright bar and restaurant offering themed dinners and entertainment.

Shopping
Alamo Trading Post: Disney memorabilia plus food and drink. More expensive than you would pay in a local supermarket.

WHERE TO STAY OUTSIDE DISNEYLAND PARIS

The main advantage of staying outside Disneyland Paris is the cost – particularly if you are a couple or single person, unable to utilise the 'rooms for four' basis that the Disney hotels operate on.

Another advantage is that it gives you the opportunity to explore the local countryside and sample the flavour of real France. Staying outside the park will give you the chance to experience French cuisine. While remaining in Disneyland Paris makes it easy to forget you are in France at all.

You can book accommodation independently or through a tour operator (see page 33). If you book independently, remember that you will have to pay to get into the park each day.

MOTELS

The nearest accommodation to Disneyland Paris is in modern rather uninspiring satellite towns. Here you will find plenty of cheap motel-type establishments (from about 150 to 350F per night). The rooms are basic but comfortable, and the motels usually have a cheap restaurant to eat in.

Most of the places below can cater for children in your room, either free or for a minimal charge. Motels, such as the Campanile range, offer good facilities for disabled people.

Although this type of accommodation will not give you much insight into French culture (motels are motels, which ever country you are in), they are perfectly adequate for a night or two, and after a long day touring round Disneyland Paris you will probably just want to go to bed.

Following are some of the best motels in the local vicinity. Prices are for the room per night, not per person.

L'ECUYER
St Thibault-des-Vignes (Tel: 64 02 02 44)
Distance from Disneyland Paris: 11 km
Small, clean, bright motel with a more intimate atmosphere than some of the larger local establishments. Communal areas are very well kept and the rooms, although very small, are adequate for a night or two. The food in the restaurant is very good – more imaginative than just steak and chips, but not too gourmet to cater for the whole family's tastes. 87F menu (47F children's menu). Parking.
365F per night (435F for a room with three beds). Children under 12 free.

BALLADINS HOTEL
Torcy (Tel: 60 17 63 09)
Distance from Disneyland Paris: 10 km
Cheap, modern hotel with free bed in your room for under twelves. Television is available at an extra 24F per night. Parking.
219F per night (Mon-Thur), 150F per night weekends.

HOTEL 1 PREMIERE CLASS
Torcy (Tel: 60 17 30 19)
Distance from Disneyland Paris: 10 km
Part of the Hotel Campanile complex in Torcy (see below). Rooms comprise a double bed, a single bunk bed, shower, wash-basin, toilet, TV and telephone. Hot and cold beverages, as well as toiletry articles are available from vending machines. You can eat cheaply at the Campanile hotel opposite or at the Côte à Côte restaurant next door. Parking.
149F per night. 32F breakfast.

HOTEL 1 PREMIERE CLASS
St Thibault-des-Vignes (Tel: 60 35 01 34)
Distance from Disneyland Paris: 9 km
New hotel with 120 rooms. Rooms comprise two
single beds and one bunk bed. Similar furnishings
and facilities to sister hotel in Torcy above.
Parking.
179F per night.

HOTEL RESTAURANT LE BEAUVAL
Meaux Beauval (Tel: 64 33 88 11)
Distance from Disneyland Paris: 16 km
A good hotel for families. Located next door to the
Place Beauval shopping complex. Prettier than
average bedrooms, each with a telephone, satellite
TV and private bathroom. Cots are provided free
of charge. Two specially designed disabled rooms.
Tiled restaurant. Breakfast 30F. Buffet menu 79F.
Children's menu 39F. High chairs available.
Parking.
220F per night (one or two people), 270F (three in
room), 320F (four in room). New Soirée Etape
package is available – 295F per person (or 385F
for two people) for one night's accommodation,
breakfast and dinner.

HOTEL CAMPANILE
Torcy (Tel: 60 17 84 85)
Distance from Disneyland Paris: 10 km
High quality chain of French hotels providing
comfortable, motel-style accommodation. This is
the nearest Campanile hotel to Disneyland Paris.
It has a 24-hour reception, plenty of parking space
and a cheap restaurant which serves dinner
(90–117F menu includes three courses and wine)

until 10 p.m. every night. Children's menu is 39F for four courses and a drink. Rooms are clean, functional and easy to reach from your car. It is a good hotel for disabled people with well-designed handicap-relieving rooms). All rooms have a TV, radio alarm, telephone and private bathroom.

If you stay here it is a good idea to prepare yourself for a long day at Disneyland Paris after their 'all you can eat' buffet breakfast!

340F per room, per night (82F for an extra bed in the room).

HOTEL CAMPANILE
Meaux (Tel: 60 23 41 41)
Distance from Disneyland Paris: 17 km

Part of the same chain as the Campanile in Torcy with a cheap restaurant and similar facilities. The advantage of staying in this one is that it is only a few minutes from the centre of Meaux, an interesting old town to explore and shop in. Breakfast 30F. Parking.

270F per night (49F for an extra bed). Children under 12 free.

HOTEL MERCURE
Saint-Witz, Fosses (Tel: 34 68 28 28 or book through their London office 0181 741 3100)
Distance from Disneyland Paris: 30 km

Another big chain of French hotels and a good place to stay if you plan to visit Parc Asterix (2 minutes away) as well as Disneyland Paris (20–30 minutes drive). Don't be put off by the cheap-looking exterior. It is actually much nicer inside. The hotel has an attractive bar area and restaurant, and 115 rooms – all with a bathroom, TV, telephone and mini-bar. There is an outdoor swimming-pool, a children's play area, and volleyball, ping-pong and short-tennis courts.

From 495F per night. 54F buffet breakfast. (Under 16s can share parents' room and have breakfast for free.)

HOTEL ACOSTEL
Meaux (Tel: 64 33 28 58)
Distance from Disneyland Paris: 17 km
Recommended. Although this motel-style hotel looks rather shabby from the road, it is actually a great place to stay, particularly in the summer. The staff are exceptionally friendly, and the clean, comfortable bedrooms open out on to the swimming-pool and overlook the River Marne. There is no hotel restaurant (although they do serve breakfast), but you will find plenty of places to eat nearby.

Parking. Play area, bikes, ping-pong, volleyball, outdoor swimming-pool. High chairs and cots available.

245F per night (room with shower), 270F (room with bath). 30F breakfast. Children under 13 are free.

HOTEL CLIMAT
Meaux (Tel: 64 33 1547)
Distance from Disneyland Paris: 18 km
This is a fairly typical local motel with 60 clean, simply decorated bedrooms. There are also rooms for disabled people. Its main feature is its restaurant – La Soupière – which is located in a separate building with an aviary of exotic birds. Menus from 85F to 125F (39F for children). Breakfast 34F.

Prices vary according to season – from 228F per night. Children under 13 years old sleep free in parents' room.

AUBERGES

If you are looking for somewhere more traditional to stay, there are several small family-run auberges in the local vicinity. These are usually more suitable for couples than families, as the rooms have not always been updated to cater for more than two.

One of the main advantages of staying in an auberge is that they often have excellent restaurants with gourmet menus – fitting in with the French principle that eating is always more important than sleeping!

Following are some of the best auberges and nearby traditional accommodation.

LE PLAT D'ETAIN
Jouarre (Tel: 60 22 06 07)
Distance from Disneyland Paris: 28 km
It is a very short drive (about 20 minutes) along the autoroute from the old village of Jouarre to Disneyland Paris. If you are looking for somewhere traditional to stay, this small auberge (part of the Logis de France chain) is ideal, with 24 well-maintained bedrooms and an exceptionally pretty dining-room with a beamed ceiling and carved, wooden chairs. Jouarre, itself, is a working market-town. The auberge is a few metres away from the market where locals barter for chickens, rabbits, lambs and other livestock. There is also an old abbey to visit a couple of minutes walk away. The auberge is more suitable for couples than families. 250F per night.

LE RELAIS GOURMAND
Crecy-la-Chapelle (Tel: 64 63 92 15)
Distance from Disneyland Paris: 8 km
This small roadside auberge is full of character
and charm, with 15 old-fashioned rooms. Downstairs is all dark wood and lace, and local painters
(including Corot) have left murals as way of pay-
ment for their board and lodging. There is a pretty
restaurant and walled garden for summer dining.
The nearby village of Crecy-la-Chapelle is one of
the prettiest and most traditional in the Disneyland Paris vicinity. Ask for a room at the back of
the building as the auberge is located by a busy
road.
More suitable for couples or single travellers than
families. Parking. Terrace.
195–220F per night. 98–165F menus.

HOSTELLERIE LE GONFALON
Germigny L'Evèque (Tel: 64 33 16 05)
Distance from Disneyland Paris: 22 km
If you want a romantic, pretty little place to
stay, with a superb restaurant, this hostellerie
is ideal. This friendly family-run hotel is set
overlooking the Marne river in a sleepy little
village, a few minutes drive away from Meaux.
There are only ten bedrooms, the best of which
have balconies overlooking the river. Rooms at
the top of the house are small. The elegant
restaurant (a popular place with locals) is
superb and, as you will guess from the big lobster tank, specialises in seafood and gourmet
food. Expect to pay double the room rate for
dîner-à-deux.
320–340F per night.

AUBERGE DU PETIT CHEVAL D'OR
Plailly (Tel: 44 54 36 33)
Distance from Disneyland Paris: 25 km
This charming roadside auberge near Ermoneville is only a few minutes from Parc Asterix and a pleasant 20–30 minute drive from Disneyland Paris. There are 28 rooms all with TV and telephone; 16 have bathrooms and five have showers. From 180–500F per night.

HOSTELLERIE DU COUNTRY-CLUB
Samois-sur-Seine, nr Fontainebleau (64 24 60 34)
Distance from Disneyland Paris: 65 km
Although it is too far to commute to Disneyland Paris every day, this is a charming riverside place to stay at if you want to extend your holiday with a day or two in the Fontainebleau country (see Chapter Thirteen: Excursions).

Located about 9 km from the hustle and bustle of Fontainebleau, Samois-sur-Seine is a quiet, pretty village full of beautiful villas, fashionable restaurants and flower-decked bridges for romantic walks. The hotel has a terrace overlooking the river, facilitating sunbathing and summer dining, and a tennis court. The rooms are small but comfortable, the staff welcoming. Parking is provided.
Menus 145–195F (children's menu 60F). Cots and high chairs are available.
380F per night (60F for an extra bed).

CHATEAUX

If you don't mind a slightly longer drive to Disneyland Paris, there are few more luxurious places to stay than in a converted château. These usually have exceptionally good restaurants and are a good base for exploring the local countryside. Following are some suggestions:

HOSTELLERIE DU CHATEAU
(Tel: 23 82 21 13)
Distance from Disneyland Paris: 90 km
A long drive to Disneyland Paris, but worth it if you want somewhere really special to stay and are only planning to spend one day at the park. The château dates back to 1206 and the ruins of the original Château de Fere, built by Robert de Dreux, grandson of Louis VI, are preserved in the grounds of the Hostellerie. Lit up at night, it makes a very romantic setting.

Families of four are automatically upgraded to a suite. The suite in the castle turret is a splendid apartment complete with a huge living area and a central jacuzzi bath! Dinner in the Hostellerie is a truly gourmet experience and one to be savoured at leisure.

In conjunction with Moët Chandon, the Hostellerie is organising special Disneyland Paris breaks which include entrance tickets to the theme park and a Champagne tour and tasting. This works out at very good value – from 590F per person for one night in a suite (including breakfast), entry into Disneyland Paris, a presentation box of Champagne, and a visit to the Moët & Chandon cellars nearby. An additional night at the Hostellerie with a two-day Disneyland Paris pass is available at a 517F supplement. Outdoor swimming-pool. Parking.

CHATEAU DE GRAND ROMAINE
Lesigny (Tel: 60 02 21 24)
Distance from Disneyland Paris: 22 km
Set in 70 acres of parkland, this château hotel has 90 rooms which are separate from the original château. Leisure facilities include two outdoor swimming-pools, five tennis courts, volleyball, golf practice nets, table tennis, sauna and games rooms. Golf courses are available nearby. Panoramic restaurant. Cots and high chairs available.
500–550F per night. Children under 12 years old free. 50F breakfast.

CHATEAU MORTEFONTAINE
Plailly (Tel: 44 54 30 94)
Distance from Disneyland Paris: 30 km
This handsome château is a little shabby at the edges, but is conveniently located for Parc Asterix, and about a 30-minute drive from Disneyland Paris. The best bedrooms are on the first floor – the ones above are rather cramped. The staff are all very friendly and speak English. There are large, uncultivated grounds at the back of this château which date back to the seventh and eighth century. Breakfast is served in the conservatory, lunch (in summer) on the terrace, and dinner (superb, nouvelle-cuisine style) in a small, panelled diningroom. 50F breakfast.
500F per night (100F for an extra bed). Cots available free of charge. Suite 950F.

CAMPING AND CARAVANNING

Apart from Disney's luxurious Camp Davy Crockett (see above) there are several campsites near the theme park. Expect to pay about 50F per night at these local sites.

To book a package with ferry crossings and insurance, contact Caravan & Camping Service in London (Tel: 0171 792 1944).

PARC DE LA COLLINE
Torcy (Tel: 60 05 42 32)
Distance from Disneyland Paris: 10 km
It is a shame that this site is located near a busy road as it has good access to the sporting facilities across the road at Parc de Loisirs (see Chapter Thirteen: Excursions). They also have chalets for rent from 450F per night (sleeps four people).

CAMP DE LA BASE DE LOISIRS DE JABLINES
Jablines (Tel: 60 26 04 31)
Distance from Disneyland Paris: 12 km
Small site near Disneyland Paris with access to leisure facilities such as bicycle hire, waterslide and golf practice.

LES BONDONS
La Ferte-sous-Jouarre (Tel: 60 22 00 23)
Distance from Disneyland Paris: 28 km
Easy access to Disneyland Paris on A4. Quiet site in grounds of a château. Caravans only.

LES USAGES
Saacy-sur-Marne (Bookings through Caravan & Camping Service; Tel: 0171 792 1944)
Distance from Disneyland Paris: Approximately 45 km
Tucked away in the countryside surrounded by

fields and overlooking the Marne Valley, this is a small, well-run site with 100 pitches about 30 minutes drive from Disneyland. Small play area for young children on site. Good range of shops, bars and restaurants in the nearby pretty town of La Ferte-sous-Jouarre.

LE PETIT BARBEAU
Samois-sur-Seine (Tel: 64 24 63 45)
Distance from Disneyland Paris: 65 km
Too far to commute to Disneyland Paris daily, but it is set in a pretty village and can be used as a base for exploring Fontainebleau as an extension to your Disney holiday.

STAYING IN PARIS

Disneyland Paris is within easy reach of Paris and many tour operators are combining accommodation in the French capital with day trips to Disneyland Paris.

The RER train network connects Disneyland Paris to five Parisian stations (Etoile, Auber, Châtelet, Gare de Lyon and Nation). The journey takes about 35 minutes from Châtelet-Les Halles.

Accommodation in Paris can be booked independently or as part of a Disneyland Paris package (see page 33). If you book independently, remember, you will have to pay entrance fees into the park each day.

HOTELS
There are thousands of hotels in Paris where you will pay from about 200F per night upwards. For a small fee, the Paris Tourist Office (Central

Welcome Service, 127 Avenue des Champs-Elysees; Tel: 47 23 61 72) can make same-day reservations for you.

SELF-CATERING
Rothray (Tel: 48 87 13 37)
Parisian apartment rental service. Seven-day minimum. All apartments are centrally located.

CAMPING DU BOIS DE BOULOGNE
Camping d'Ile de France, Bois de Boulogne (Tel: 45 24 30 00)
The only major campsite in the Paris area. Unfortunately, you cannot make advance bookings and there are huge queues every morning in the summer – if you want a space, make sure you get there early.

CHAPTER FIVE

THE LAYOUT OF DISNEYLAND PARIS

In order to make the most of your visit, it is important to familiarise yourself with the layout of the park before you go (see map).

This chapter includes brief descriptions of the five themed lands and lists everything they have to offer, including services, such as stroller rental and lost property. We have highlighted (★) particularly interesting attractions in each land.

For detailed reviews of rides and attractions see Chapter Six, for restaurants Chapter Seven, for shops Chapter Eight and for entertainment see Chapter Nine. For suggested tours see Chapter Twelve.

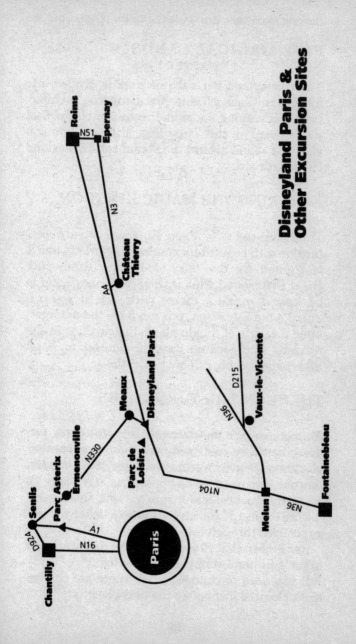

Disneyland Paris & Other Excursion Sites

FIVE MAGICAL LANDS

The Disneyland Paris theme park is divided into five lands – each with its own distinctive architecture, landscaping, shops and restaurants. The best way to explore this is by foot, although you can also ride round aboard the steam-run Disneyland Paris Railroad.

ENTERING THE MAGIC KINGDOM

The entrance to the Magic Kingdom is truly spectacular with beautifully manicured gardens, and it is fronted by the fairytale-looking candy-pink Hotel Disneyland. This is the first Disney hotel to be located inside a theme park, and if you can afford a top-rate room, you can have the unforgettable pleasure of flinging back the curtains in the morning and looking straight out on to Main Street and Sleeping Beauty's Castle.

THROUGH THE TURNSTILES

As you approach the electronic turnstile gates, you are greeted by cast members inquiring whether you already have an entrance ticket. If not you can buy one, two or three-day passports at a booth. To avoid the queues, make sure you get there early (before 9 a.m.). If you already have a ticket you can go straight through into the park.

Remember that if you exit in the day, you need to get your hand stamped for re-entry.

If you need to change money, there are change kiosks located just before the ticket booths.

Other facilities outside the gates include Guest Storage and Guests Relations (general information kiosk).

MAIN STREET, USA

Best land for:
- Shopping
- Architectural detail
- Tea and cakes
- Entertainment

Your visit to Disneyland Paris will inevitably start in Main Street, USA. Disney music uplifts you the minute you walk through the gates. Main Street, USA is one of the most aesthetically pleasing parts of the park, a pollution-free Utopia where the walls of the pretty, candy-coloured painted buildings are never graffitied and the pavements are spotlessly clean.

Main Street takes you back to turn of the century small-town America and is a hubbub of activity with individually designed traditional shops and the smells of home-baked cookies and old-fashioned eating establishments.

The architectural detail is tremendous. Make sure you look up at the buildings as you walk down the street. Above Main Street Motors, for example, you can actually see the coffee cup steaming in the old Nescafé poster!

If it is your first day at Disneyland Paris, you will probably want to walk slowly up Main Street, USA. On later occasions you may enjoy jumping aboard one of the main old vehicles that travel up and down the street, such as the horse-drawn street-car which takes you down to Sleeping Beauty's Castle.

Services in Main Street, USA

Babycare/Lost Children Centre
Next to Plaza Gardens Restaurant at the Central Plaza end of Main Street. Facilities for preparing formulas, warming bottles, breast-feeding and changing nappies. Disposable nappies and a limited selection of baby foods are available. There are also high chairs for feeding babies in peace and quiet. If you lose your child you should report it here or at City Hall. For further information tel: 64 74 30 00.

City Hall
Information centre and place to pick up maps and entertainment timetables. This is also the location of Lost and Found and the place to report lost children. (Tel: 64 74 30 00)

First Aid
Next to Plaza Gardens Restaurant on Central Plaza. (Tel: 64 74 30 00)

Foreign Currency
Located at Park Entrance and at City Hall.

Lost and Found
City Hall, Main Street, USA. (Tel: 64 74 30 00)

Lost Children
City Hall, Main Street, USA, or Lost Children office in the Babycare Centre, next to Plaza

Gardens Restaurant at the Central Plaza end of Main Street.

Lockers
Located underneath the station. Operated by a 10F piece, they are big enough to store handbags or small parcels.

Camera Rentals
Town Square Photography, Main Street, USA. Cameras and videos for hire.

Photo Processing
Town Square Photography, Main Street, USA. Very expensive. Wait until you get home!

Strollers and Wheelchairs
Town Square Terrace. 30F plus 20F refundable deposit. You will be doing a lot of walking during the day so it is definitely worth hiring a pushchair even for slightly older children (three or four years old), who will quickly tire themselves out through all the excitement.

Rides and Attractions
Disneyland Paris Railroad ★
Main Street Vehicles
Horse-drawn street-cars

Shops
Plaza West Boutique
Plaza East Boutique
The Storybook Store ★
Ribbons & Bows Hat Shop
Emporium

71

Town Square Photography
Silhouette Artist
Boardwalk Candy Palace
Disney Clothiers, Ltd
Harrington's Fine China & Porcelains ★
Disneyana Collectibles
Disney & Co
Glass Fantasies
Main Street Motors
Dapper Dan's Hair Cuts

Eating and Drinking

Table-Service
Walt's ★

Self-Service
Plaza Gardens Restaurant ★

Fast-Food
Victoria's Home-Style Cooking ★
Casey's Corner ★
Market House Deli ★

Snacks and Refreshments
The Ice-Cream Company
The Coffee Grinder
Cookie Kitchen
Cable-Car Bake Shop ★
The Gibson Girl's Ice-Cream Parlour

Entertainment
The Disneyland Paris Band
The Disney Parade ★
Electrical Parade ★

FRONTIERLAND

Best land for:
- Sitting in the sun and soaking up the Wild West atmosphere
- Playing cowboys and Indians
- Shopping for Wild West goods

Frontierland brings to life the legends of the American frontier with a landscape inspired by Monument Valley, Utah and the Gold Rush. This is the best land to be in on a sunny day as there are all sorts of trips on the rivers of the Wild West and there is lots to watch if you just want to sit down and relax.

Rides and Attractions

Mark Twain or Molly Brown Steamboats
Phantom Manor ★
Rustler Roundup Shootin' Gallery
Big Thunder Mountain Railroad ★
River Rogue Keelboats
Indian Canoes
Cottonwood Creek Ranch
Legends of the Wild West
Frontierland Depot – Disneyland Paris Railroad
The Chaparral Stage

Shops

Tobias Norton & Sons ★
Bonanza Outfitters ★
Eureka Mining Supplies
Pueblo Trading Post
Woodcarver's Workshop

Eating and Drinking

Table-Service
Silver Spur Steakhouse
The Lucky Nugget Saloon ★

Fast-Food
Last Chance Café
Fuente del Oro
Cowboy Cookout Barbeque ★

Entertainment
Lucky Nugget Revue ★

ADVENTURELAND

Best land for:
● Exotic atmosphere at night
● Young explorers

This is the most exotic land with an exquisitely designed eastern bazaar, and a tropical island which children will love to explore. Make sure you wander round this land at night, when the torchlights and Moroccan-style buildings are tremendously atmospheric.

Rides and Attractions
Adventure Isle ★
Swiss Family Robinson Treehouse ★
Pirates of the Caribbean ★
Indiana Jones and the Temple of Peril ★
Le Passage Enchanté d'Aladdin.

Shops
Indiana Jones Adventure Outpost

Adventureland Bazaar
– Le Chant des Tam-Tams
– Les Trésors de Schéhérazade
– La Reine des Serpents
– L'Echoppe d'Aladin
– La Girafe Curieuse
– Le Coffre du Capitaine ★

Eating and Drinking

Table-Service
Blue Lagoon Restaurant ★

Fast-Food
Colonel Hathi's Pizza Outpost ★

Snacks and Refeshments
Café de la Brousse
Captain Hook's Galley

Entertainment
Tam-Tams Africains ★

FANTASYLAND

Best land for:
● Little children
● Fairground-style rides

Fantasyland is the prettiest and most magical
land at Disneyland Paris. If you are travelling
with young children, you will want to spend most
of your time here. The highlight of Fantasyland
and Disneyland Paris is the stunningly ornate
Sleeping Beauty's Castle.

Rides and Attractions

Sleeping Beauty's Castle ★
Snow White and the Seven Dwarfs
Pinocchio's Adventures
Lancelot's Carousel
Peter Pan's Flight ★
Dumbo the Flying Elephant
Mad Hatter's Tea Cups
Alice's Curious Labyrinth
It's A Small World ★
Casey Junior – Le Petit Train du Cirque ★
Le Pays des Contes de Fées
Les Pirouettes du Vieux Moulin

Shops

La Boutique du Château
Merlin L'Enchanteur
La Confiserie des Trois Fées
La Chaumière des Sept Nains
Sir Mickey's
La Bottega di Geppetto
La Petite Maison des Jouets

Eating and Drinking

Table-Service
Auberge de Cendrillon ★

Fast-Food
Pizzeria Bella Notte ★
Au Châlet de la Marionnette ★
Toad Hall Restaurant

Snacks and Refreshments
Fantasia Gelati
March Hare Refreshments
The Old Mill

Entertainment
C'est Magique (Fantasy Festival Stage) ★

DISCOVERYLAND

Best land for:
● Teenagers

This land is the smallest of the Magical Kingdom lands, which will, no doubt, become much more popular with the opening of Space Mountain in June 1995. There's a lot of exciting attractions here, and the futuristic architecture is designed in the way that old inventors such as Jules Verne and Leonardo da Vinci would have envisaged it.

Rides and Attractions
Le Visionarium ★
Orbitron
Autopia
Star Tours ★
Captain EO (CinéMagique) ★
Les Mysteres du Nautilus ★
Space Mountain ★

Shops
Constellations
Star Traders ★

Eating and Drinking

Fast-Food
Café Hyperion ★

Entertainment
Beauty and the Beast (Videopolis) ★

FESTIVAL DISNEY

Festival Disney is the entertainment centre, a few minutes walk from the park. The most attractive part about it is its location on the edge of Lake Buena Vista. Otherwise it is rather a dreary, uninspiring place.

Following is a list of its facilities. For reviews of restaurants see page 144, shops page 169 and entertainment page 184.

Services
Post Office
Boat Rental
Tourist Office
Arcade

Shops
The Disney Store
Team Mickey
Mattel World of Toys
Hollywood Pictures: Boutique Lion King
Buffalo Trading Company

Eating and Drinking

Table-Service
Annette's Diner ★
Los Angeles Bar & Grill
Key West Seafood ★
The Steakhouse

Fast-Food
Carnegie's ★

Bars
Sports Bar ★
Billy Bob's Bar
Rock 'n' Roll Bar ★

Entertainment
Buffalo Bill's Wild West Show ★
Hurricane's Disco
Billy Bob's Country and Western Saloon

INFORMATION DIRECTORY

Services and Facilities

Babycare Centre
Changing tables, bottle warmers and feeding area
available next to Plaza Gardens, Main Street, USA.

Baby-sitting
Available in all the hotels.

Boat Rental
Boats can be hired outside the Steakhouse
(Festival Disney).

Camera Rentals
Still and video cameras for rent at Town Square.

Car Rental
Europcar have an office near the Hotel Santa Fe
and car hire can be booked through the hotels.

Cash Machines
In Liberty Arcade and Discovery Arcade (Main
Street, USA).

Children's Pushchairs
Can be rented at Town Square Terrace in Main Street, USA.

Currency Exchange
Available at the Main Entrance, Main Street Station, Frontierland Depot and in Adventureland and Fantasyland. Money can also be changed in the hotels and in the Post Office.

Disabled Facilities
Special Services Guide available at City Hall (Main Street, USA).

First Aid
Next to Plaza Gardens Restaurant (Main Street, USA).

Lockers
Coin-operated lockers at Main Street Station. Larger items can be stored at Guest Storage, outside the Main Entrance.

Lost Child
Report to City Hall or Lost Children next to Plaza Gardens in Main Street, USA.

Lost and Found
At City Hall in Main Street, USA.

Pets
Pets are not allowed in the park (apart from guide dogs). They may be left at the Animal Care Centre near the carpark.

Picnic Area
Located between the carpark and Disney Square.
You are not allowed to bring food or beverages into
the park.

Postboxes
Postboxes are located throughout the park.

Post Office
Located in Festival Disney.

Sporting Facilities

Golf
Open mid-March to mid-November.

A 27-hole golf course, located 5 km from the
theme park. The 90-hectare course consists of
three nines, which can be played in a number of
combinations. Each nine has four teeing grounds
and is rated at Par 36.

Facilities comprise a 40-position driving range,
a putting green which is in the shape of Mickey
Mouse ears, a clubhouse with restaurant, a pro
shop, and a club and repair service. There is also a
conference room, guest showers and lockers, elec-
tric golf cart rental, shoe and club hire, and lessons
are available. For more information and reservations, tel: 60 45 68 04.

Swimming-pools
Located at Disneyland Hotel, Hotel New York, the
Newport Bay Club, the Sequoia Lodge and Camp
Davy Crockett.

81

Ice Skating
Available at Hotel New York.

Croquet
Available at Hotel Newport Bay Club.

Health Clubs
Can be found at Disneyland Hotel, Hotel New York, Newport Baby Club and Sequoia Lodge.

Cycling and Pony Rides
Can be enjoyed at Camp Davy Crockett, and pony rides are also available at Hotel Cheyenne.

CHAPTER SIX

REVIEWS OF RIDES AND ATTRACTIONS

So, you are finally at Disneyland Paris and cannot wait to try out all the rides! In this chapter we review every ride and attraction in the theme park. These are arranged under the various lands.

We have given every ride a star rating (* to *****) so that you can make an instant decision about whether you want to do this one or not. As some of the rides may be superb fun for older children but terrifying for little ones, we have indicated age suitability in our reviews. We have also included suggestions of the best time of day to do the ride and an estimated queuing time, although bear in mind that this will vary according to the time of year (see page 33 – when to go). Rides are suitable for disabled people and pregnant women, unless stated otherwise.

After reading this chapter, you will have a good idea about the rides you will want to try. If your time at Disneyland Paris is limited (one or two days) we suggest you turn to Chapter 13 (page 234) and follow one of our suggested itineraries. These tours have been specially designed to help you avoid the queues and see the best parts of the park.

Unfortunately, the weather in Disneyland Paris is not reliable. If you are caught in a downpour, turn to Chapter Eleven (page 199) for tips on what to do when it rains.

The park has been reviewed in a clockwise direction, starting in Main Street, USA.

MAIN STREET, USA

DISNEYLAND PARIS RAILROAD

Location: Main Street, USA.

Overall comment:
A fun and restful way to see the whole of the park. A tame ride that is well worth doing, particularly with young children.

Star Ratings:
Adults ***
Teenagers ***
7–12 year olds ****
4–7 year olds *****
Toddlers *****

Description:
This is the first ride you see in Disneyland Paris, a steam train that chugs its way round the 2.2 km perimeter of the park, at a slow, leisurely pace.

Like everything at Disney, the attention to detail is superb. Old-fashioned prams and leather luggage wait to be 'boarded' and attendants on the platform warn you that shooting buffalo from the train is strictly prohibited! There are three trains, all reproduced from a late nineteenth-century design.

The 20-minute journey is an excellent way of acquainting yourself with the size and general layout of the park, although your view is somewhat restricted, particularly at night.

The train chugs to a halt three times, at Frontierland, at Fantasyland and again at Discoveryland. It is more than just a train ride as you pass through a superb depiction of the Grand Canyon complete with wildcats frolicking in the sun and a wolf howling from a jagged peak. You also enter a grotto world full of skeletons and buried treasures – this might be too scary for little children if the train wasn't playing such jolly music.

Make sure you wrap up warmly, particularly if you ride the train at night. As the sides of the train are open, keep a close eye on excitable toddlers.

The trains run every 15–20 minutes. Don't make the mistake of thinking you have to use the train to get around the park, as Disneyland Paris is much smaller than it first appears and, if queues are long, it is quicker to walk.

Duration of ride: 25 minutes.

Length of queues: Up to 45 minutes.
If the queues extend on to the street, come back later, or board the train at Fantasyland, Frontierland or Discoveryland.

Entertainment during queuing:
Apart from the amusing comments from station-

master, the nineteenth-century style station platform is a good vantage point to look down on
everything happening on Town Square.

Best time of day to go there:
First thing in the morning as it is a good way of
getting your bearings.
   Last ride of the day as a final memory of the park.

Visual and audio effects:
Fun, especially the Grand Canyon Diorama. Commentary in English, French, German and Italian.

Worth another ride?
Yes, this is a good ride to do again at the end of
your visit.

MAIN STREET VEHICLES

Location: Main Street, USA.

Overall comment:
Various types of old-fashioned transport taking
you from Town Square to Central Plaza.

Star Ratings:
Adults *
Teenagers *
7–12 year olds **
4–7 year olds ****
Toddlers *****

Description:
There are all sorts of old-fashioned vehicles

which will transport you down Main Street, USA. These include a horse-drawn streetcar, a fire truck, a limousine and an old-fashioned paddy wagon. They are all fun for little children and for anyone with tired feet, although they are not worth queuing long for. For a good view of the street, jump aboard the double-decker Omnibus and keep your eyes peeled for all the detail on the buildings in the street. The vehicles act as one-way transportation between Town Square and Central Plaza.

Length of queues: Usually minimal.

Entertainment during queuing:
Watching everything that is going on in Town Square. There is often a brass band playing.

Best time of day to go there:
Any time.

Worth another ride?
Toddlers may enjoy it so much that they'll insist on going again!

FRONTIERLAND

BIG THUNDER MOUNTAIN RAILROAD

Location: Frontierland.

Overall comment:
One of the best 'thrill' rides in Disneyland Paris, with added special effects, offering superb views of Frontierland – if you've got your eyes open!

Star Ratings:
Adults *****
Teenagers *****
7–12 year olds *****
Under 7 year olds *** (Only for the bolder and older children in this group. There is a height restriction of 1.02 m.)
Toddlers: Not suitable.
Also not suitable for pregnant women or anyone with back, neck or muscular problems.

Description:
All aboard the runaway mine train on this wild roller-coaster ride. Although the ride is quite tame by fairground standards, you'll still get a lurching stomach in the first few hair-raising seconds. The Wild West landscape is superbly detailed with animatronic asses, a goat which tugs the jeans from a miner's washing line and a howling coyote. Be prepared to be splashed (but not soaked) when the train plunges through the water.

Duration of ride: 3 minutes.

Length of queues:
This is one of the most popular rides in Disneyland Paris, although the queues are better now that there are two other roller-coaster rides (Indiana Jones and Space Mountain) in the park. Nevertheless, you may still have to queue for over an hour at peak times. This is not one to queue for on a rainy day, however, as only about 15 minutes of this wait is under cover. Adults will not mind waiting as there is lots to see from the vantage

point – like the Phantom Manor queue you are up high, enabling you to watch the activity below. Children may get fidgety as there is no organised entertainment, but the ride is so good they are bound to queue again and again!

Entertainment during queuing:
None.

Best time of day to go there:
First thing in the morning or during the parade.

Visual and audio effects:
Superb.

Worth another ride?
Definitely! – but if you ride again immediately, it may not be as thrilling. Come back and do it again at the end of the day – the ride takes on a new dimension in the dark.

MARK TWAIN AND THE MOLLY BROWN STEAMBOATS

Location: Frontierland.

Overall comment:
A good ride on which you can take some spectacular photographs. Relaxing on a sunny day, but otherwise dull and dreary. One for the grannies.

Star Ratings:
Adults ***

Teenagers *
7–12 year olds ***
4–7 year olds ****
Toddlers ***

Description:
The Molly Brown and Mark Twain paddle-steamers take you on a slow, unadventurous voyage around Big Thunder Mountain on the Rivers of the Far West. It may not be a thrill a minute, but it is a good opportunity to photograph the geysers and other sculpted areas, and it is very atmospheric and evocative of the era.

Make for the mid-deck (front) bow area and try to get a seat – most people bound straight up to the top only to find all the seats have gone. If it's raining, there are indoor seated cabins, but this really is a ride to try on a sunny day. It can also be quite romantic at night as a way of relaxing after dinner.

Duration of ride: 12 minutes.

Length of queues: Up to 20 minutes.
Most people in the sheltered waiting area should board the paddle-steamer. If queues are big, don't bother.

Entertainment during queuing:
None, apart from watching the screaming crowds on Thunder Mountain.

Best time of day to go there:
When it is sunny or for relaxation after dinner.

Visual and audio effects:
Most of the commentary and dialogue is in French.
The action is 'on-shore' – you watch from the ship.
Don't stand too near the funnel or you will be
blasted by the ship's horn.

Worth another ride?
No.

RIVER ROGUE KEELBOATS

Location: Frontierland.

Overall comment:
Similar appeal as Mark Twain and Molly Brown
Steamboats. Don't bother doing both these rides
on the same day.

Star Ratings:
Adults ***
Teenagers*
7–12 year olds ***
4–7 year olds ****
Toddlers ***

Description:
Styled like nineteenth-century keelboats, this is
another way to explore the Rivers of the Far West.
There are two wooden boats, the *Coyote* and the
Raccoon. Both are powered by diesel engines and
are steered by Disney cast members who stand at
the back, dressed in long coats, leather boots and
big black hats.

91

Duration of ride: About 8 minutes.

Length of queues: Up to 45 minutes on a hot day.

Entertainment during queuing:
None.

Best time of day to go there:
When it's sunny. But don't waste time queuing.

Visual and audio effects:
Like the steamboats, all the action is on-shore.

Worth another ride?
No.

INDIAN BIRCHBARK CANOES

Location: Frontierland.

Overall comment:
A more active way to explore the Rivers of the
Far West. Relaxing on a warm day. Fun for chil-
dren.

Star Ratings:
Adults ***
Teenagers **
7–12 year olds ****
4–7 year olds ****
Toddlers **

Description:
This is a paddle around the island in a fibreglass canoe. You sit in pairs with the cast members (one at front and one at back) guiding you. Everyone has a paddle, although you get the feeling that the canoe is mainly being propelled along by the paddles of the cast members. On a warm, sunny day it's a relaxing way to view Disneyland Paris's detailed landscaping on the shore (watch out for the old-timer relaxing with his barking dog), and to watch the antics of the Railroad. This form of river transport also enables you to take a closer look at the island.

Duration of ride: About 10 minutes.

Length of queues: Up to 45 minutes.
(Not worth queuing for more than 20 minutes.)

Entertainment during queuing:
None.

Best time of day to go there:
When it's warm.

Visual and audio effects:
Only those animatronics onshore and on the island.

Worth another ride?
No.

PHANTOM MANOR

Location: Frontierland.

Overall comment:
Don't miss this!

One of the best and most imaginative of Disneyland Paris's attractions. Not a high-speed thrill ride, but one to be savoured again and again.

Star Ratings:
Adults *****
Teenagers *****
7–12 year olds *****
4–7 year olds *** (Not admitted without an adult. Too scary for small or nervous children.)
Toddlers * (Too scary.)

Description:
Phantom Manor is a large, forbidding Victorian house on the top of a hill overlooking the Rivers of the Far West. As you approach its doors, you can hear the wind howling and you'll notice how everything in the garden has withered.

A crowd of about 30 are shown into a doorless chamber, a room that eerily elongates itself and where a bolt of lightning reveals that someone – or something – is watching you! You are told that in this room a death has occurred. There is no way out. You must move on to a 'doom buggy', a carriage for two which swivels round 180 degrees as you tour the haunted manor.

If you do not like the feeling of creepy crawlies, you will be glad to know that there are no unseen

94

'things' touching you. The scariness is purely visual and aural. The wedding reception scene is particularly haunting.

If you survive the doom buggy journey, leave the manor and turn left to the 'Crypt' to see the Boot Hill Cemetery (look out for the morbidly funny epitaphs) and to oversee the Hot Springs. This is a good vantage point for photos of the lake – can you spot the coyote on the opposite hill?

Duration of ride: 15–20 minutes.

Length of queues: Up to 40 minutes. (Most of the queuing is under cover.)

Entertainment during queuing:
None. But you can watch the Molly Brown Steamboat and the Big Thunder Mountain Railroad. The grounds of the manor are also superbly detailed with gnarled and withered trees, the sound of a howling wind, and tiles and cracked paint peeling off the eerie house.

Best time of day to go there:
Any time.

Visual and audio effects:
Disney's finest show of audio-animatronics and visuals, surpassed only by Pirates of the Caribbean.

Worth another ride?
Yes, if only to work out how they do it!

RUSTLER ROUNDUP SHOOTIN' GALLERY

Location: Frontierland.

Overall comment:
The only attraction inside Disneyland Paris which is not included in your passport. It costs 10F for a rifle – a bit steep for what is just an ordinary side-show.

Star Ratings:
Adults *
Teenagers **
7–12 year olds **
Under 7 year olds: Not allowed.

Description:
A standard fairground electronic shooting gallery – hit the bullseye and you activate the exhibit, in this case, a Wild West frontier scene with exploding dynamite and little foxes popping their heads out of holes.

Like similar electronic games, this is liable to malfunction. Some of the gun coin-slots will be taped up. Make sure you put your coin in the right slot and not in that of your neighbour's gun.

For 10F you get an indeterminate number of bullets. However, it is difficult to perceive whether you or your neighbour have actually hit the target.

Length of queues: Up to 10 minutes.

Entertainment during queuing:
None.

Best time of day to go there:
Any time, but don't bother queuing.

Visual and audio effects:
Disappointing special effects (you'll get better on Brighton Pier!). The kick from the gun isn't satisfying enough either.

Worth another go?
No. Not worth paying for.

COTTONWOOD CREEK RANCH

Location: Frontierland.

Overall comment:
Ideal for little children who can stroke their favourite farmyard animals in this spotlessly clean corral.

Star Ratings:
Adults *
Teenagers *
7–12 year olds ***
4–7 year olds ****
Toddlers ****

Description:
Cottonwood Creek Ranch is a small, corralled area in which sheep, goats, rabbits, chickens and piglets can be viewed and stroked in a scrupulously clean environment. The rabbit hutch is spacious but has an unattractive grilled floor. The farmyard animals are run-of-the-mill but look

healthy and well groomed. Most of the animals are allowed to roam free and will nuzzle your hand for food.

Only go and see this attraction if you have time to spare, or if your youngsters have never touched a farmyard animal. Make sure the animals don't chew your camera/handbag!

You are not allowed to feed the animals and strollers must be left outside.

Duration of visit: As long as you like.

Length of queues: None.

Best time of day to go there:
Any time. Closes at dusk.

Visual and audio effects:
None, just the real grunts and bleats of the animals!

Worth another visit?
No.

LEGENDS OF THE WILD WEST

Location: Frontierland.

Overall comment:
Fans of the Wild West will enjoy the chance to see how the cowboys lived.

Star Ratings:
Adults **

Teenagers **
7–12 year olds **
4–7 year olds **
Toddlers *

Description:
A series of static tableaux depicting scenes from the Old West, including a disappointingly deserted Indian reservation. There are a lot of steps to be climbed, so it's not for the elderly or the very young.

Duration of visit: As long as you want.

Length of queues: Minimal.

Entertainment during queuing:
None.

Best time of day to go there:
Any time.

Visual and audio effects:
None – these waxworks don't bat an eyelid!

Worth another visit?
No.

ADVENTURELAND

PIRATES OF THE CARIBBEAN

Location: Adventureland.

99

Overall comment:
Don't miss this! It's even better than the same ride in Florida.

An outstanding indoor boat ride through various audio-animatronic tableaux of pirate scenes. Good mix of humour and thrills – Disney 'imagineering' at its best.

Star Ratings:
Adults *****
Teenagers *****
7–12 year olds *****
4–7 year olds ***** (More for the older children in this category. Younger ones may be scared.)
Toddlers: Not suitable.
Also not suitable for pregnant women due to the plunging motion of the boats under attack.

Description:
Board the boat and travel through a succession of pirate scenes. Enter into the depths of the pirates' underground lair, past tableaux of skeletons and shipwrecked timbers.

At the beginning of the journey you glide past the Blue Lagoon restaurant where human diners feast on tropical food. Then it's off to watch the merry audio-animatronic crew chasing maidens, fighting over treasure and swigging from barrels of liquor. Watch out for the eerie eyes (bats/rats) peering at you from dark corners.

This fabulous ride offers roller-coaster thrills too. Your boat hurtles down two slopes, escaping cannon fire. A pirate swings on a rope over your heads.

Don't take children who scare easily, although

the ever-present jolly pirates' song lifts the spirits.

Keep your arms inside the boat and expect to be splashed a little.

Duration of ride: 12 minutes.

Length of queues: Up to one hour.
Allow 25 minutes if you join end of queue at the entrance. On a hot day, queuing for this ride can be sweaty and claustrophobic.

Entertainment during queuing:
Jolly yo-ho-ho music, eerie sound effects, pirate tableaux.

Best time of day to go there:
Early, as queues will be smaller and you will probably want to go back and do it again.

Visual and audio effects:
Disney's best audio-animatronic ride; rich in atmosphere and packed with thrills.

Worth another ride?
Definitely.

ADVENTURE ISLE

This is divided into two islets joined by bridges. In the north is Treasure Island, in the south is The Swiss Family Robinson Tree-House. See reviews below.

TREASURE ISLAND

Location: Adventureland.

Overall comment:
Based on Treasure Island by Robert Louis Stevenson and Peter Pan by J.M. Barrie, both Scottish novelists.

Great fun for young explorers. Older children can play here while parents have coffee in Captain Hook's galley.

Star Ratings:
Adults **
Teenagers **
7–12 year olds *****
4–7 year olds *****
Toddlers ***

Description:
This island is great fun for children who will enjoy clambering over the precarious bridges and exploring the network of tunnels and underground caves. Walk up to Spyglass Hill which has a series of vantage points offering a panoramic view of Adventureland (don't forget to take your camera). Young children will enjoy the shuddering suspension bridge, overlooking the wrecked galleon. Look through the brass telescopes at each vantage point.

Afterwards, descend into Ben Gunn's Cave to see the stalactites and stalagmites. Or feel your way around Dead Man's Maze, a spooky underground network of tunnels beneath a spectacular waterfall, illuminated by glowing bats' eyes.

Peter Pan fans will enjoy visiting Captain

Hook's Pirate Ship. There is a café in the ship or you can take your camera upstairs on deck and let the children play with the ship's wheel and rigging. Near the ship you will see the sinister Skull Rock where you can look across at Captain Hook's Ship through the eye sockets of the 'rock'.

Duration of visit: Allow half an hour to explore.

Length of queues: None.

Entertainment during queuing:
None.

Best time of day to go there:
Any time.

Visual and audio effects:
A few tableaux and spooky lights in the mazes, but most are natural.

Worth another visit?
Not unless you have spare time at the end of your visit.

SWISS FAMILY ROBINSON TREE-HOUSE

Location: Adventureland.

Overall comment:
Based on *Swiss Family Robinson* by Johann David Wyss, this is the tree-top home built by the ship-wrecked Robinson family. A fine example of Disney imagineering.

Star Ratings:
Adults ****
Teenagers ****
7–12 year olds *****
4–7 year olds ****
Toddlers * (too many steps to contend with)
Not suitable for people who have problems walking or climbing stairs.

Description:
This 90-foot tree, in the heart of Adventureland, is a miracle of Disney imagineering as it is entirely man-made, from its roots to its leaves. Based on the 1960s real-life Disney adventure film, this depicts the house built by the Robinsons when they were shipwrecked on their desert island. The rooms are packed with detail, such as the old books and maps in the library, and the water wheel and water supply which are fashioned from bamboo.

It really captures the imagination of what living in a tree-house could be like and makes you realise how lucky the Robinsons were to have salvaged so much undamaged furniture from their ship. The climate must have been a far cry from Parisian temperatures for the Robinsons to have endured an open-air bedroom!

Afterwards it's also fun to explore the Root Cellar (La Ventre de la Terre), a dark maze under the roots of the tree. Lit by flickering lamps, it's difficult to see where you are walking and you are likely to bump into people. In the centre, you can look up at the tree-house. Not for the claustrophobic or those who are afraid of the dark!

Duration of visit: Allow 20 minutes to walk slowly round.

Length of queues: Queuing is rare, although you may have to wait for up to 15 minutes at the entrance if people congest inside.

Entertainment during queuing:
None.

Best time of day to go there:
Any time, preferably not right at the end of the day when you feel too weary to walk to the top!

Visual and audio effects:
None, apart from the visible engineering.

Worth another visit?
Not really.

LE PASSAGE ENCHANTE D'ALADDIN

Location: Adventureland.

Overall comment:
Based on the animated feature film *Aladdin*, this is a series of tableaux scenes from *Aladdin* – enjoyable in a similar way to looking at Selfridge's window displays at Christmas time.

Star Ratings:
Adults **
Teenagers **
7–12 year olds **

4–7 year olds ***
Toddlers ****

Description:
This is a small, low-key attraction that is good to
visit as a break from some of the high-thrill rides
such as Indiana Jones. It will also appeal to young
children and *Aladdin* fans. You walk through a
cave and watch mainly static models behind glass
screens depicting scenes from the film. Tame stuff
but charming all the same.

Length of queues: None.

Entertainment during queuing:
None.

Best time of day to go there:
Any time. Good in the rain as it's under cover.

Visual and audio effects:
Piped music and songs from the film. The evil
tiger's head is quite terrifying!

Worth another visit?
This may be one of your young child's or toddler's
favourite attractions, so be prepared to be dragged
back in several times!

**INDIANA JONES AND THE TEMPLE OF
PERIL**

Location: Adventureland.

Overall comment:
Exciting roller-coaster-thrill ride based on the run-
away mining train from the *Indiana Jones and the
Temple of Doom* movie. Don't miss this!

Star Ratings:
Adults *****
Teenagers *****
7–12 year olds ***** (Children under 8 years old
not allowed. Height restriction of 1.40 m.)
4–7 year olds: Height restrictions
Toddlers: Not suitable.
Also not suitable for pregnant women or anyone
suffering from heart, back or neck problems.

Description:
Although it feels far too short for serious white-
knuckle fans, this ride is more exciting than
Thunder Mountain Railroad, and the first
downward plunge will have your stomach churning. Take away the props and the atmospheric
music and this would be a very ordinary roller-
coaster ride. But, as usual, Disney's imagineers
lift it above the ordinary with a series of tableaux
depicting Indiana Jones's deserted camp; the
inevitable palm trees; carved lions and cobras
guarding the Temple of Peril; and some reassur-
ingly sturdy mining cars with padded body-pro-
tectors to restrain you. It's probably the best view
of the park and surrounding countryside – if you
can keep your eyes open!

Duration of ride: 2½ minutes.

Length of queues: 45–75 minutes.

Entertainment during queuing:
Static tableaux of scenes from *Indiana Jones* movies.

Best time of day to go there:
Early in the morning or during the parades.

Visual and audio effects:
Music while queuing. Once on the ride, however, the thrills are enough.

Worth another ride?
Definitely!

FANTASYLAND

SLEEPING BEAUTY'S CASTLE

Location: Fantasyland.

Overall comment:
Don't miss this! A stunningly designed castle and the central landmark of Disneyland Paris, it is based on *Sleeping Beauty* by Frenchman Charles Perrault.

Star Ratings:
Adults ****
Teenagers ****
7–12 year olds ****
4–7 year olds ****
Toddlers *** (avoid the cellar, if you think your child may be frightened by the dragon)

Description:

This beautifully ornate and magical castle is the central landmark of Fantasyland and Disneyland Paris, and is a worthwhile attraction in itself. It is based on a European castle, complete with tapestries, vaulted ceilings, a moat, a waterfall and a cellar where a gruesome dragon lurks.

Children will never be content with a tour of your average European castle after this! Beautifully designed inside and out, you can experience the story of *Sleeping Beauty* through hand-painted storybooks, ornate tapestries and stained-glass windows. In typical Disney style, the central oval stained glass over the Gothic archway magically changes scenes.

Don't forget to go downstairs to the dragon's lair where a smoke-breathing, red-eyed dragon raises its ugly head from a pool; a broken chain dangling from its neck, its long tail flicking menacingly.

Length of queues: None.

Best time of day to go there:

As you don't have to queue for this attraction, don't waste time touring the castle when you first arrive at the park. Come back and walk round at your leisure when the other rides are busier.

Visual and audio effects:

The animatronic dragon is a treat – a deep-throated roar and acrid smoke adds to the chilling effect. The castle has also been specially designed with forced perspective so that the tallest tower (45 m) looks much taller than it actually is.

Worth another visit?
Yes, it's even more atmospheric and beautiful at dark.

SNOW WHITE AND THE SEVEN DWARFS

Location: Fantasyland.

Overall comment:
Based on the German fairytale by the Grimm brothers. This is more interesting than next door's Pinocchio's Adventures but too scary for very little children. These two rides are very similar, so choose one or the other depending on your child's age and sensitivity – and the length of the queues!

Star Ratings:
Adults ***
Teenagers **
7–12 year olds *****
4–7 year olds ***** (smaller, sensitive children may be scared)
Toddlers * (too scary)

Description:
A fast-moving indoor ride in seated trolleys named after the Seven Dwarfs. This is a great ride for children with enough detail to keep adults amused. You pass through a series of rooms depicting scenes from the *Snow White* film. Parents be warned: the ride concentrates on the wicked witch and some scenes, particularly the one in the forest where it looks as though you are going to be entangled by the evil trees, are truly terrifying! The ride

moves a little too quickly for adults who will be disappointed not to have more time to take in all the intricate details. You may want to ride again while junior wants to run off next door to see Pinocchio!

Duration of ride: 3 minutes.

Length of queues: Up to 45 minutes.

Entertainment during queuing:
None.

Best time of day to go there:
Early, while others are still lingering in Sleeping Beauty's Castle, or during the Parade.

Visual and audio effects:
Great creepy sound effects and jolly tunes from the film. After the colourful imagery of the opening tableaux (like the Pinocchio ride), most of the scenes are dark and gloomy – almost like a mystical Ghost Train ride.

Worth another ride?
Yes, it's all over too quickly!

PINOCCHIO'S ADVENTURES

Location: Fantasyland.

Overall comment:
Based on the Italian fairytale by Carlo Collodi. Similar to Snow White and the Seven Dwarfs (see

page 110) but less scary, so it is more suitable for little children. Choose one or the other depending on your child's age and sensitivity – and the length of the queues!

Star Ratings:
Adults ***
Teenagers **
7–12 year olds ****
4–7 year olds *****.
Toddlers ** (Very small children may be scared.)

Description:
Great ride for the under-sevens, especially if they've seen the film and know the story and characters. Not as scary as Snow White, but again the ride concentrates on the more frightening scenes from the film, such as the scenes of the fairground, the puppeteer's cages and the whale. Very young children may be wailing by the time they get off.

Duration of ride: 3 minutes.

Length of queues: Fast-moving. Allow 15 to 20 minutes if busy.

Entertainment during queuing:
None.

Best time of day to go there:
Early, while people are still lingering in Main Street, USA, or Sleeping Beauty's castle, or during the Parade.

Visual and audio effects:
Starts with jolly tunes, giving way to scary sound effects once in the fairground scene. The best effect is of the whale raising its head to swallow you (despite a warning from Jiminy Cricket).

Worth another ride?
Yes, if it's your child's favourite story.

PETER PAN'S FLIGHT

Location: Fantasyland.

Overall comment:
Don't miss this!
   At last, you too have a chance to fly like Peter Pan over the rooftops of London. Based on *Peter Pan* by J. M. Barrie, this is a visually thrilling ride that adults will enjoy as much as children.

Star Ratings:
Adults *****
Teenagers ****
7–12 year olds *****
4–7 year olds ***** (must be accompanied by an adult)
Toddlers *** (may be scared)

Description:
This is one of the most popular rides at Disneyland Paris, and once children have tried it they usually want to do it again and again. The reason for its success is that it really does make you feel as though you are flying in a pirate ship above the

rooftops and twinkling lights of London. The ship is suspended from above and whisks you through a series of tableaux from the *Peter Pan* film. Standing in the children's bedroom, you are whisked out of the window, through the clouds to Never-Never-Land.

Magical. Disney at its best.

Very small children may, however, have problems seeing over the edge of the ship and also may find the crocodile scene scary.

Duration of ride: 4 minutes.

Length of queues: Up to 1½ hours at peak times. (This is one of the worst rides in Disneyland Paris for queuing.)

Entertainment during queuing:
None.

Best time of day to go there:
If you are with children, go as soon as you get to the park, otherwise during the Parade. A good time for adults is late at night, just before the park closes.

Visual and audio effects:
Visually one of Disney's best rides in Fantasyland.

Worth another ride?
Yes, definitely!

LE CAROUSEL DE LANCELOT

Location: Fantasyland.

Overall comment:
A beautifully ornate merry-go-round, delightful for children on a sunny day, but miserable when it is wet and windy.

Star Ratings:
Adults **
Teenagers *
7–12 year olds **
4–7 year olds ****
Toddlers *****

Description:
This colourful carousel adds to the carnival/fairground atmosphere of Fantasyland. The horses are beautifully ornate with gold manes. Their flanks are embossed with brightly coloured gems and their hooves with shoes of silver, bronze or shiny gold. This is, allegedly, Elizabeth Taylor's favourite ride.

The horses on the outside are the grandest. Toddlers seem to love this ride and leather straps are provided to hold them tight.

Be careful: children who are at the end of the queue may be disappointed to end up in one of the carriages – large semi-circular seated areas between the horses.

As there is so much of novelty value elsewhere, don't waste time queuing for what is basically an ordinary, traditional fairground ride.

Duration of ride: 90 seconds.

Length of queues: Up to 15 minutes on a sunny day.

Entertainment during queuing:
None.

Best time of day to go there:
Any time. After dark is particularly romantic.

Visual and audio effects:
Disney songs set to carousel arrangements.

Worth another ride?
No.

DUMBO THE FLYING ELEPHANT

Location: Fantasyland.

Overall comment:
Traditional high-flying fairground ride with a Dumbo theme. Great fun for little ones.

Star Ratings:
Adults **
Teenagers *
7–12 year olds ***
4–7 year olds ***** (Must be accompanied by an adult.)
Toddlers ***** (Must be accompanied by an adult. Under-ones are not allowed. Some toddlers may be scared.)

Description:
Take to the skies with big-eared Dumbo, under the supervision of Timothy Mouse who conducts the flight standing on the top of a hot-air balloon.

116

There are sixteen flying baby elephants, each seating two passengers. You control how often your Dumbo flies up and down.

Similar ride to Orbitron, aimed at small children but without the visual impact of Orbitron's design.

Duration of ride: 2 minutes.

Length of queues: Up to 45 minutes.

Entertainment during queuing:
None.

Best time of day to go there:
Any time.

Visual and audio effects:
None.

Worth another ride?
Yes, for children. Also fun at night.

MAD HATTER'S TEACUPS

Location: Fantasyland.

Overall comment:
Traditional fairground ride, based on *Alice in Wonderland* by Lewis Carroll, with giant cups which whirl you round.

Star Ratings:
Adults ***

Teenagers ***
7–12 year olds ****
4–7 year olds *****
Toddlers ****
Not suitable for pregnant women.

Description:
Eighteen giant teacups (which can hold a family of five) whirl round in circles under a covered pagoda decorated with Chinese lanterns. The teacup spins one way while the saucer turns in the opposite direction. You have some control over the spinning speed, but this is not one to do after a big meal or ice-cream!

This ride offers more thrills than Dumbo or Autopia and so is more popular with children up to mid-teens.

One to head for if it's wet – even the queuing is under cover.

Duration of ride: 90 seconds.

Length of queues: Up to 20–30 minutes.
(Less than for most of the other rides in Fantasyland.)

Entertainment during queuing:
None.

Best time of day to go there:
Any time, but preferably not after eating!

Visual and audio effects:
Fairground music.

Worth another ride?
No, but young children may drag you on again!

ALICE'S CURIOUS LABYRINTH

Location: Fantasyland.

Overall comment:
Based on *Alice in Wonderland* by Lewis Carroll.
An outdoor, walkthrough attraction for all the family, and an ideal spot to take photos. Low on thrills; more one to do at leisure.

Star Ratings:
Adults ****
Teenagers **
7–12 year olds ****
4–7 year olds ****
Toddlers ***

Description:
This outdoor attraction is easily ignored by those queuing for the carriage rides at the entrance to Fantasyland, but it is great fun for the under-12s. It is not a complex maze in the style of Hampton Court, but more a corridor between real hedges and through plastic ivy arches, leading to the Queen of Hearts' castle at the centre.

Children will love the squeaks and whistles from the hedges and the Alice characters peering at them from corners. The vantage points from the castle also offer what must be the prettiest picture opportunities of all in Disneyland Paris, so do not forget your camera.

Don't worry if you hate the frustration of wrong turnings in mazes – it's impossible to get lost in this one and it offers a pleasant stroll through mostly real greenery.

Duration of visit: Allow 20 minutes.

Length of queues: Up to 20 minutes at peak times.

Entertainment during queuing:
None.

Best time of day to go there:
Any time, but preferably when it is sunny.

Visual and audio effects:
A few noises from hidden speakers in the hedges. But, disappointingly, few of the characters move.

Worth another visit?
No.

IT'S A SMALL WORLD!

Location: Fantasyland.

Overall comment:
A leisurely boat ride through a world of beautifully costumed singing and dancing dolls. A good ride for the whole family to do together. Don't miss this!

Star Ratings:
Adults ****
Teenagers **

7–12 year olds ****
4–7 year olds *****
Toddlers *****

Description:
It's a Small World! was designed by Walt Disney to be 'The happiest cruise that ever sailed round the world.' Your cruise starts at London Bridge and travels through the five continents. This is the sort of ride that you either love or hate. Thrill-seekers will find it deadly dull, but they may enjoy the chance to do something with the rest of the family. Most people, however, can't help being enchanted by the musical dolls who are lavishly costumed in the style of their country. The song they sing is one of those infuriating ones that can never be forgotten! Young children will find it educational to identify which countries the dolls are representing. It is also a cosy ride to do on a cold day.

After disembarking from your indoor world cruise, you can spend another couple of minutes walking through a village of model houses. The idea is that you peer through the windows and watch the different uses of the telephone in modern society. Although this is a blatant plug for sponsors France Telecom, it is fun for very little children as the windows are arranged at different heights so that they have to squat down to look through the ones near the floor, and ask their parents to lift them up so they can see through the ones in the tall buildings.

Duration of ride: 7 minutes.
Allow another five to ten minutes to look round the houses.

Length of queues: Fast-moving.
Allow 30 minutes at peak time.

Entertainment during queuing:
None.

Best time of day to go there:
Any time, but if it looks busy, go back during the
Parade.

Visual and audio effects:
Nothing very sophisticated, but the dancing dolls,
in their wonderfully detailed national costumes,
are a feast for the eyes.

Worth another ride?
Yes.

LES PIROUETTES DU VIEUX MOULIN

Location: Fantasyland.

Overall comment:
Good vantage point for photos of Fantasyland.
Otherwise, rather dull.

Star Ratings:
Adults *
Teenagers *
7–12 year olds **
4–7 year olds ***
Toddlers ***

Description:
A small, traditional ferris wheel which turns round and round like a Dutch windmill. Passengers are seated in oversized wooden buckets. Not very exciting but good place to take photos.

Duration of ride: 1½ minutes.

Length of queues: Minimal.

Entertainment during queuing:
None.

Best time of day to go there:
When there are no queues.

Visual and audio effects:
None.

Worth another ride?
No.

CASEY JUNIOR

Location: Fantasyland.

Overall comment:
Based on the circus train in *Dumbo*. A little circus train takes you on a journey through scenes from your favourite fairytales. Magical for small children and those with tired feet.

Star Ratings:
Adults ***

123

Teenagers **
7–12 year olds ***
4–7 year olds ****
Toddlers ****

Description:
All aboard Casey Junior's Circus Train which puffs
around the miniature villages of Storybook Land!
This offers very gentle roller-coaster thrills for
small children as it travels up and down over little
arches in the track. The whole family will enjoy the
intricately detailed villages of Storybook Land
with its quaint sets and scenes from *Aladdin*,
Beauty and the Beast, *Snow White and the Seven
Dwarfs*, *Peter and the Wolf* and *Rapunzel*.

Duration of ride: 2½ minutes.

Length of queues: 20–30 minutes.

Best time of day to go there:
Early in the morning or during the Parade.

Entertainment during queuing:
None.

Audio and visual effects:
Music to accompany the various stories depicted.

Worth another ride?
You can see the same scenes from a boat in Les
Pays de Contes des Fées.

LE PAYS DES CONTES DE FEES

Location: Fantasyland.

Overall comment:
Gentle boat cruise through Storybook Land. Fun for small children.

Star Ratings:
Adults **
Teenagers **
7–12 year olds ***
4–7 year olds ****
Toddlers *****

Description:
View the same miniature scenes from international folklore and classic Disney animated films that you can see from Casey Junior's train-ride – this time gliding along in a canal boat.

Duration of ride: 4 minutes.

Length of queues: 10–15 minutes.

Best time of day to go there:
Early in the morning or during the Parade.

Entertainment during queuing:
None.

Visual and audio effects:
Music accompanying the passing scenes.

125

Worth another ride?
No.

DISCOVERYLAND

STAR TOURS

Location: Discoveryland.

Overall comment:
Don't miss this! Superbly thrilling ride based on George Lucas's *Star Wars* movies.

Star Ratings:
Adults *****
Teenagers *****
7–12 year olds *****
4–7 year olds ** (Should be accompanied by an adult. Small children may be scared. Height restriction 1.02 m.)
Toddlers: Not suitable. Children under three are not allowed.
Not suitable for pregnant women or anyone who suffers from back, neck, heart or muscular problems.

Description:
This ride owes much to the imagination of Disney and of the film-maker George Lucas. Disney has employed Lucas's characters and sets, as well as incorporating the thrilling music and effects of his *Star Wars* movies, to create all the thrills and spills of being a passenger on one of the spaceships. The ride uses a specially made film of a journey into space in which you take part.

Before boarding your ship (each of the six ships has a capacity for 40 people), you are briefed for three minutes about safety instructions. The dialogue for this is in French with English subtitles. The doors slide open and you enter your ship, take your seat and fasten your belt.

A robot welcomes you as your pilot and the screen shield lifts to reveal a film screen. The android speaks French, although there are also brief interruptions from the Control Centre in English.

You soon find out that this is your robot pilot's first flight! Be prepared for a lot of thrills and spills as you are rocketed into space with your inexperienced pilot trying to manoeuvre you past meteorites and all sorts of adventures, including an inter-galactic battle.

Some people feel more secure in this sort of ride than the open thrill rides, such as Thunder Mountain, as it's evident that it's simulated. Others may feel claustrophobic and trapped in a chamber. Not advisable for anyone suffering from motion sickness.

Duration of ride: 6 minutes.

Length of queues: Up to an hour and a half at peak times. Expect 15 minutes from the first robot tableau.

Entertainment during queuing:
Queuing takes place indoors through corridors of an orbital space station where you watch moving androids repairing spaceships. Dialogue is in French and English.

127

The queue is slow-moving but there is lots of atmosphere with airport-style announcements over the Tannoy and spacecraft debris to look at in a futuristic space-repair-shop setting.

As in the movies, the robots are cute and witty.

Best time of day to go there:
First thing.

Visual and audio effects:
The visual effects are superb, both while queuing and during the ride. The film effects are first rate, as befits the stature of the *Star Wars* movies.

Worth another ride?
Yes. Several! Although you must expect the overall sensation to be diminished with repeated rides. The first ride is always the best!

L'ASTROPORT SERVICES INTERSTELLAIRES

Location: Discoveryland.

Overall comment:
High-tech playground of interactive games.

Star Ratings:
Adults ***
Teenagers ***
7–12 year olds ***
4–7 year olds ***
Toddlers *

Description:
Located inside the Star Tours adventure, this is a high-tech playground with five interactive games which work with voice recognition and touch-sensitive screens. Guests are welcomed by ROX-N, a multilingual audio-animatronic android, who introduces you to each game in English, French, German, Italian and Spanish. One of the most amusing games is having your passport photo taken at the Photomorph. This allows you to modify your human identity by distorting eyes, ears, nose, etc – you can purchase a photo of your new cosmic look at the IBM InfoPoint at the exit. The Star Course game is also fun and welcomes 11 aspiring space pilots to take part in a kind of space-age bumper-car game.

Duration of visit: As long as you wish.

Length of queues: Minimal.

Best time of day to go there:
After doing Star Tours.

Visual and audio effects:
Highly sophisticated interactive machines.

Worth another visit?
If it grabs you.

LE VISIONARIUM

Location: Discoveryland.

Overall comment:
Don't miss this! Superb 360-degree surround-vision film, more scenic than thrilling.

Star Ratings:
Adults *****
Teenagers *****
7–12 year olds ****
4–7 year olds ***
Toddlers: Not suitable.

Description:
This is one of the few attractions which has been especially devised for Disneyland Paris and not just imported from the States. This 360-degree film is packed with European influences and references to its great inventors, as well as containing some great footage of European towns and countryside.

Have a rest and a snack before queuing for Le Visionarium as you will be on your feet for half an hour inside.

Queuing is half undercover, before you are shown through the doors into a waiting area – not empty like Captain EO, but facing a wall of video screens. This is La Banque de l'Image. Flying machines, ships, undersea vessels, spacecraft and astronauts all hang from the ceiling, while a wall display shows inventions of the last century. The room is a celebration of the works of H.G. Wells and Jules Verne. A countdown digital clock shows the time lapsing until show time (8 minutes before the auditorium doors open). Meanwhile, the wallscreen shows images of transport from years gone by.

Your host is the Timekeeper who introduces you to his robotic friend, 9-Eye. You are shown into a large circular room with the nine film screens which are used to portray the film footage as seen by 9-Eye.

There are no seats and you stand in rows with your own headset should you need to listen to the dialogue in English, German or Italian.

The Timekeeper then takes you and Jules Verne (played by actor Michel Piccoli) on a journey back through time, starting with the Dinosaur Age and moving into the future. The impact of the film is outstanding and you really feel as though you are travelling through time, even though you are standing still. The glimpse of Paris in 100 years' time is overwhelming, and the detail in the film demands you see it a second time. (One niggle is a hillside battle which we are told is between the Scots and the Brits!) The film stars Jeremy Irons and Gerard Depardieu.

Duration of visit: 30 minutes.

Length of queues: Up to 20 minutes.

Entertainment during queuing:
None outside, but there is a film in the waiting area.

Best time of day to go there:
Any time.

Visual and audio effects:
Excellent film effects along the lines of Circlevision at Epcot, in Florida. More scenic than thrilling.

Worth another visit?
Definitely, as there is so much detail to absorb.

CINEMAGIQUE: CAPTAIN EO

Location: Discoveryland.

Overall comment:
Raucous 3-D film which will delight fans of
Michael Jackson, *Star Wars*, or both.

Star Ratings:
Adults ***
Teenagers *****
7–12 year olds *****
4–7 year olds *** (may be scared by the villainess
who resembles a cross between a giant spider and
Freddy Krueger!)
Toddlers: Not suitable.
Not suitable for people with sensitive hearing.

Description:
A 20-minute 3-D film and pastiche of *Star Wars*,
starring a crew of cuddly animals, a curiously
gruff robot styled as a one-legged metallic
Admiral, Michael Jackson as Captain EO and
Anjelica Huston as the Supreme Leader.

The storyline takes EO and his crew into battle
with an enemy craft, before crash-landing on a for-
eign planet and coming face to face with an array
of villains.

The 3-D effects are augmented by flashing lights
set in the ceiling of the auditorium, surround-
sound and a searchlight which at one point sweeps

the audience. The 3-D glasses handed out at the entrance can be fitted over your own specs.

Adults may find it too loud and young children may be frightened. Connoisseurs of pop videos will feel they've seen it all before but perhaps not at this volume, or, of course, in 3-D.

Disappointing for the French that no effort has been made to dub the dialogue into their own language – although the story itself is almost irrelevant when set against the effects.

Reviewer's tip: When filing into the auditorium, people will inevitably sit down in the middle, despite being told to move right along (viewing of the film is the same from all seats). The only way to deal with these people is simply to squeeze past.

Duration of film: About 20 minutes.

Length of queues: Up to one hour at peak times.

Entertainment during queuing:
None, and it's mostly outdoors and jolly miserable in the wet. Take a brolly and a poncho.

Best time of day to go there:
Any time.

Visual and audio effects:
Great 3D, although it doesn't seem to be in sharp focus. It all adds up to an extended pop video for Jackson. The main song is one specially written for this film – a rather repetitive pop chant – but he closes with his popular 'Another Part of Me'. It's all

very loud, and the dialogue (which is entirely in English) is not always easy to make out.

Worth another viewing?
No.

SPACE MOUNTAIN

Location: Discoveryland.

Overall comment:
Based on Jules Verne's science fiction classic *From the Earth to the Moon*, this is a sensational new ride, opening 1 June 1995, which launches you into space after catapulting you through a cannon at breathtaking speed. Different and even more exciting than Space Mountain in Florida.

Star Ratings:
Adults *****
Teenagers *****
7–12 year olds ***** for those tall (1.40 m height restriction) and brave enough to try.
4–7 year olds: Not suitable, although they may enjoy watching the ships whizz past.
Toddlers: Not suitable.
Not suitable for pregnant women, or anyone suffering from heart, neck or back problems.

Description:
You won't be able to miss this new attraction as you'll hear a bang and see the smoke rise every time the cannon fires. This is a high-thrill indoor ride designed to simulate the experience of

launching into space. You start by walking through a starry galaxy to board your Victorian rocket-powered space ship. Once seated, a harness lowers over you. Then hold on tight for an incredibly dramatic start as the rocket is blasted from stationary position at the bottom to the top of the cannon in less than two seconds flat! From here, you're on a journey of spatial acrobatics with loops and turns. As always with Disney, you can expect surprises, such as exploding astral mines and raining meteorites. This is Disneyland Paris's highest thrill ride and for those who think their stomach can't take it, there's the option just to walk through with the people queuing and watch the rocket whizz past at speeds of up to 70 km per hour.

Duration of ride: 2½ minutes.

Entertainment during queuing:
Watching the rockets zoom past indoors and walking through space.

Best time of day to go there:
As soon as gates open or during the parade.

Visual and audio effects:
The visual effects are designed to create the feeling of travelling in space. The audio effects are superb. Each passenger has speakers by his or her head and the music has been specially choreographed so that it changes with the action in the ride.

Worth another ride ?
Definitely.

LES MYSTERES DU NAUTILUS

Location: Discoveryland.

Overall comment:
Based on Captain Nemo's submarine and Jules
Verne's world of *20,000 Leagues Under the Sea*
this is a self-guided tour of Captain Nemo's undersea vessel, *Nautilus*. You pass through his elabo-
rate living quarters, the operations room and end
up in a thrilling close encounter with a giant
squid.

Star Ratings:
Adults *****
Teenagers ****
7–12 year olds ****
4–7 year olds ***
Toddlers * (The realistic visual effects and loud
noise of the squid attack will be too scary.)

Description:
The undersea version of the Swiss Family
Robinson tree-house. This self-guided tour of the
undersea vessel, *Nautilus*, is wonderfully detailed,
with turn-of-the-century interiors (the captain's
bed, bookcases and map room) housed in the
atmospheric surroundings of the gun-metal-grey
submarine. Recorded shouts from an unseen crew
(all French) and the gruff commentary from Nemo
lend the atmosphere of a bustling sea voyage.

You're invited to sit on small, wooden steps in the Grand Salon from where you can view the exciting battle with the giant squid taking place behind the glass porthole.

Duration: 10–15 minutes.

Length of queues: 20–30 minutes.

Entertainment during queuing:
Captain Nemo's treasure is on display in a glass case. And you can admire the atmospheric dank surroundings of the long, metallic corridor.

Best time of day to go there:
Any time.

Visual and audio effects:
Top marks for recreating the claustrophobic atmosphere of a submarine with hisses of steam, yelling crewmates – and, of course, the impressive octopus attack.

Worth another visit?
Yes, as there is so much detail.

ORBITRON

Location: Discoveryland.

Overall comment:
An average fairground ride; low on thrills but beautifully designed.

Star Ratings:
Adults **
Teenagers **
7–12 year olds ***
4–7 year olds ****
Toddlers **

Description:
Fairground-goers will no doubt have come across this type of flying machine/spaceship ride before. Twelve ships, each with a capacity for three passengers (at a squeeze), travel round a globe. Press the control lever forward to go up, pull it towards you to descend.

As it only lasts a couple of minutes, you won't be bored, but it has little to offer the thrill-seekers. Children will enjoy pulling the lever back and forwards to create an up and down ride as you whizz past the beautifully ornate metallic 'moons' of Orbitron.

Duration of ride: 2 minutes.

Length of queues: Up to 45 minutes at peak time. The ride can take, on average, only 24 people per two minutes.

Entertainment during queuing:
None.

Best time of day to go there:
Any time.

Visual and audio effects:
More a visual spectacle for onlookers. Once

aboard, there isn't much sensation at all, and the outlook on to the park is nothing special.

Worth another ride?
No.

AUTOPIA

Location: Discoveryland.

Overall comment:
Boring for adults, but a chance for children to take the wheel of a futuristic car and drive it round a curving rail-track.

Star Ratings:
Adults *
Teenagers ***
7–12 year olds ****
4–7 year olds *** (There is a height restriction for this ride.)
Toddlers: Not suitable for very little children. Under-ones are not allowed.
Not suitable for pregnant women, people with back, neck or muscular problems.

Description:
The main appeal of this ride is that it enables children and teenagers to drive an open-topped, racing-style two-seater car in total safety around a curving rail-track. Adults who have a driving licence, will find it frustratingly slow and rather dull! The only control is the drive-pedal which can't be called an accelerator as there is only one

speed – slow! You don't really need to steer, as there's a metal rail under the car guiding you. It's not even as much fun as dodgems, because you are not allowed to nudge the car in front.

Duration of ride: Two minutes.

Length of queues: Up to 30 minutes.
Allow 15 minutes from the circular seated area.

Entertainment during queuing:
None, apart from watching the cars go round.

Best time of day to go there:
Any time.

Visual and audio effects:
A satisfying engine roar when you press the pedal, but little to see apart from some futuristic billboards lining the track.

Worth another ride?
No.

CHAPTER SEVEN

THE UNOFFICIAL
RESTAURANT GUIDE

Eating out is always an important part of any holiday and Disneyland Paris has earned the reputation of charging exceptionally high prices for food. Thankfully, however, prices have been considerably reduced since the park first opened and eating at Disneyland Paris need no longer put you out of pocket – providing you know what's on offer.

In this chapter we help you budget your eating bills by giving you tips on eating out, reviewing all the restaurants in the park and suggesting the best value and most interesting places for you to go. We have also reviewed the restaurants in Festival Disney and highlighted the best places to eat in the hotels. Please note that all prices and menus are subject to change.

RESTAURANT TIPS

The most economical approach is to grab snacks from the speciality carts and eat in the fast-food restaurants in the park. In the summer months, you can make the most of your entrance pass by staying in the park to eat because, if you eat early (6.30 p.m. – 7 p.m.), you can then do your favourite rides again at night.

The menus and prices of the restaurants in the park have changed considerably since opening in 1992. For example, you can now buy a small burger for just 8F, whereas the cheapest burger in the park used to be 30F. Admittedly, the new 8F burger is smaller and not of such good quality, but at least it fills up hungry stomachs at a more reasonable cost.

There are now lots of fast-food restaurants at Disney, charging similar prices to what you'd pay at somewhere like McDonalds in Paris. Standard Disney fare now includes burgers, chips, hot-dogs, pizzas, sandwiches and the occasional baked potato. Sadly, most of the more interesting food outlets, such as the stall that used to make stir-fry wok dishes, have disappeared. Desserts are also monotonous – mainly chocolate brownies, giant cookies, doughnuts or fruit salad – although they are all delicious.

If the walk around the park has built up your appetite, take advantage of the set menus in the fast-food restaurants as these are good value. For example, the Donald meal costs 30F and includes a burger, chips and a drink. The children's menus are also good value – 25–32F buys a Disney carton which contains a main course, a drink, a dessert and a 'surprise'. Set-meal prices like these can save you up to 13 per cent off the price.

Feel free to sit at any of the tables on the restaurant terraces, whether you are eating there or not. Unlike Paris, there is no charge at Disney to just sit down, soak up the sun, and watch the world go by.

The portions in the fast-food restaurants are usually small, encouraging you to 'graze' throughout the day. Try to stagger your eating times so that you avoid the lunchtime crush (12.30 p.m. – 2 p.m.). If you want to eat at a table-service restaurant, make your reservation in person after 11 a.m. There is a new policy stating that tables cannot be reserved for the busy period between noon and 2.30 p.m. – so if you want to book, you'll have to eat earlier or later than this.

Have your coffee breaks in the fast-food restaurants and snack bars (6F for a coffee). You will pay twice this in the plusher establishments such as Plaza Gardens.

If budget permits, do try one of the four table-service restaurants as the quality and atmosphere in these is really good. Opt for their 140F menu, which includes three courses and a mineral water, or treat yourself to an epicurean feast with the Menu Oscar (260F) which includes a glass of champagne, three courses, a mineral water and coffee. (Children's menus cost 45F.) All the table-service restaurants now serve wine or beer with your meal. Beers cost from 20F and a 50cl carafe of wine costs 5F.

Finally, you are not allowed to bring food or drink into the park. Be warned: they have been known to search your bags! Picnic areas are located outside the park, near the carpark, although it is doubtful that you will want to leave the park during the day. If you do, make sure you get your hand stamped for re-entry.

TOP RESTAURANTS

Following is our personal selection of the best places to eat at Disneyland Paris.

BEST FOR BREAKFAST

All the hotels serve a continental breakfast (55–75F) which is often included as part of your package. If you want to eat something more substantial try the following:

Parkside Diner
Hotel New York
110F (55F children)
Worth going to for their American Breakfast which gives you a choice of pancakes with maple syrup, scrambled eggs with sausage and hash browns, smoked salmon and sour cream on a toasted bagel, or a delicious toasted granola cereal served with yoghurt and a giant bowl of fruit salad. Also includes fresh fruit juice, croissants and bread, and a choice of coffee, tea or hot chocolate.

Chuckwagon Café
Hotel Cheyenne
Good place for a reasonably priced, substantial breakfast. Like all the meals here, breakfast is a self-service affair with the food laid out on various carts. Breakfast dishes include steaming hot porridge, large bowls of fresh fruit and berries, and pancakes with maple syrup.

Cable-Car Bake Shop
Main Street, USA
If you want to have a quick breakfast in the park, you can grab a coffee and croissant or muffin at this Main Street bakery.

Character Breakfasts
Hotel Disneyland or Key West in Festival Disney.
140F (105F for the under-tens)
These are buffet breakfasts with special appearances from Disney characters.They are a real treat for the children and a good feast for the adults. Expect to see two or three characters during your hour-long breakfast. If you are starving hungry, this represents good value because you can help yourself to as much as you want from the lavish buffet. (Dishes include scrambled eggs, smoked salmon, sausages, hash browns, bacon, cereals, yogurts and a wide selection of fruits.) Young children particularly enjoy this type of breakfast as they get a chance to see their favourite characters before the day has even begun.

BEST FOR LUNCH

Food Carts
The quickest and cheapest way to eat in the park is to grab a snack from a food cart. Expect to pay 13F for a small hot dog, 15F for a jacket potato and 10–15F for popcorn. In bad weather you can buy similar fare at Victoria's Homestyle Cooking (Main Street, USA).

Victoria's Homestyle Cooking
Main Street, USA
One of the prettiest and quietest counter-service restaurants. Now serves small portions of tasty food, similar to what you buy from the food carts. Good place to come on a cold, wet day.

Walt's
Main Street, USA
Very pleasant to eat on the terrace on a sunny day.

Plaza Gardens
Main Street, USA
Self-service restaurant with high-quality food and beautiful furnishings. Live jazz at lunchtime.

Casey's Corner
Main Street, USA
The most atmospheric place to come for hot dogs and chocolate brownies. Seating inside and out. Popular with teenagers.

Pizzeria Bella Notte
Fantasyland
Fast-food pasta and pizza restaurant. Small, but tasty portions.

Colonel Hathi's
Adventureland
Located in the beautiful building that used to be the Explorer's Club table-service restaurant. Now, fast-food pasta and pizza are provided to fill you up after the thrills of the Indiana Jones ride.

Café Hyperion
Discoveryland
Giant, tiered restaurant – good for taking cover in the rain. Don't miss the Beauty and the Beast Show which is shown here every lunchtime. Standard fast-food fare of burgers or sandwiches.

Carnegie's
Festival Disney
Cheapest place for lunch if you are shopping in Festival Disney. Eat in or take away. Sandwiches and fast-food, such as quiches, are served.

Lucky Nugget Saloon
Frontierland
Western lunch while you watch a show. Fun for all the family.

BEST FOR DINNER

Blue Lagoon
Adventureland
Moonlit Caribbean-style restaurant; perfect for romantic twosomes.

Auberge de Cendrillon
Fantasyland
Pretty restaurant with Cinderella's carriage on the terrace. The nearest you'll get to a French meal at Disneyland Paris.

Key West
Festival Disney
Large, seafood restaurant overlooking Lake Buena Vista, specialising in crab dishes.

Chuck Wagon Café
Hotel Cheyenne
This is the best place for a reasonably priced family supper in a fun, Wild West atmosphere.

Crockett's Tavern
Camp Davy Crockett
Small pine-decked restaurant serving excellent burgers, with a fresh salad bar, and other simple fare for family dinners.

A GUIDE TO THE RESTAURANTS IN THE THEME PARK

All the table-service and self-service restaurants have been awarded a star rating (* to *****). This is based on the atmosphere, service and quality of food.

As the fast-food restaurants are now so uniform in design, there is little point in grading them, therefore, what follows is simply an indication of the type of food and prices to expect.

MAIN STREET, USA

Table-Service Restaurants:

Walt's
*Star Rating ****
Set menus 140F, 175F or 260F (45F children)
Closed on Wednesdays and Thursdays*
According to our waiter, this is the top restaurant in Disneyland Paris and, certainly, the food and service was of a high standard. It is an elegant restaurant; divided into several small, intimate,

themed dining-rooms. We sat upstairs in
Frontierland, an old-fashioned Wild West style
reading-room with Red Indians on the wall and
leather-bound Wild West books on the shelves. The
intimate atmosphere is enhanced by candlelight,
taped violin music and swagged velvet curtains.
Children may find the atmosphere rather formal,
but the staff are exceptionally friendly and good
with babies.

Starters cost from 35 to 62F and include smoked
salmon, coquilles Saint Jacques, and tomato and
basic soup. Main courses cost from 80 to 120F and
include roast salmon and a grilled fillet of Angus
beef with pepper sauce and lamb cutlets. Desserts
cost from 33 to 44F and include a chocolate and
custard flan, and an orange sorbet with pineapple
and mint.

The restaurant also has a terrace outside.

Self-Service Restaurants:

Plaza Gardens
*Star Rating ****
*Prices from 65 to 88F. Set menu 140F (45F chil-
dren)*
This is a very elegant, Victorian-style restaurant with buffet service. Velvet-backed chairs,
cream and gilt pillars, cloth serviettes and silver
cutlery make this the smartest self-service
restaurant in Disneyland Paris. The food is
excellent whether you want a light lunch or a
three-course dinner. Prices, however, are high,
and you pay twice as much for a coffee here as
you do at any of the fast-food restaurants. It
also gets very busy at lunchtime so try to come

early (11.30 a.m.) or after the midday crowds (2 p.m.).

Main dishes on the menu include Caesar salad, poached salmon platter, grilled chicken breast, roast veal, Maryland crabcakes and sirloin steak. Their Dauphine potatoes are delicious and could easily constitute a meal on their own. Desserts include meringues, chocolate mousse and fresh-fruit shortcake.

Warm and comfortable on a cold wet day. There is jazz at lunchtime and a terrace for eating out-side in the summer.

Fast-Food Restaurants:

Market House Deli

Old-fashioned deli which specialises in giant, freshly made sandwiches with hot pastrami (28F) or ham and cheese (18F). As it is centrally located on Main Street, queues for this restaurant are often very big. Sandwiches can also be bought from food carts, from Café Hyperion (Discoveryland) or from the Old Mill (Fantasyland).

Victoria's Homestyle Cooking

This is one of the most attractive fast-food restau-rants in Disneyland Paris and, as it is slightly tucked out of sight at the top of the Discovery Arcade, it doesn't get as busy as some of the other Main Street restaurants.

It's a good place to come on a cold, wet day as it's always warm and cosy. In the summer you can eat outside on the terrace.

The inside of the restaurant is decorated like a

pretty Victorian boarding house. It now sells the sort of snack food you would buy from the food carts, such as baked potatoes (15–20F), quiche (18F), pizza (18F) or lasagne (36F). Desserts include brownies (12F), cookies (9F) or doughnuts (10F).

Casey's Corner

Teenagers will particularly enjoy this atmospheric hot-dog haunt with its baseball-themed decor. The hot dogs here are so good, it is even busy at breakfast-time! Seating inside and out.

The menu includes hot dogs (13F or 23F), cheese dogs (23F), chicken dogs (23F), and crisps (5F). Desserts include brownies (12F). If this is crowded, hot dogs can also be bought at Café Hyperion in Discoveryland.

Snacks:

The Ice-Cream Company

Small ice-cream kiosk in Discovery Arcade.

The Coffee Grinder

Small coffee bar in Discovery Arcade.

Cookie Kitchen

Small stall with service both from the Main Street counter and inside the Cable-Car Bake Shop. Freshly baked muffins (8F), brownies (12F), cookies (9F) and coffee (6F). In cold weather you can sit and eat these in the Cable-Car Bake Shop, which is in same building. If you're with a crowd or ravenous family, you can buy a box of four cookies and three muffins for 50F.

Cable-Car Bake Shop

Old-fashioned, San Francisco-style bake shop. Good place to come for afternoon tea. Warm and cosy in the winter. Freshly baked croissants and cakes. Coffee.

The Gibson Girl's Ice-Cream Parlour

Old-fashioned ice-cream parlour at the top of Main Street with tables both inside and out. Ice-cream cornets (15F), yoghurt ice-cream cone (16F), chocolate and pistachio ice-cream sandwich (10F). A good place to position yourself before the Parade.

FRONTIERLAND

Table-Service Restaurants:

The Lucky Nugget Saloon

*Star Rating ***
Set menu 80F adults (40F children)
Closed on Wednesdays and Thursdays
A reasonably priced menu and a great show make this a good place to come for lunch. The room is beautifully designed as a revue hall, with tables on the floor at the front for groups of three or more, and counter seats behind for couples or those on their own.

The menu includes chicken wings with barbeque sauce, chilli con carne, hot beef tortilla, French fries and a chocolate brownie. Wines and beers are available with your meal.

The 30-minute revue show (see page 187 for review) takes place every day, except Wednesday and Thursday.

Silver Spur Steakhouse
Star Rating ***
Set menus 140F, 175F or 260F (45F children)
Closed on Wednesdays and Thursdays
This is a plain, old-fashioned steakhouse with no entertainment to keep the kids amused. The decor is plush with chandeliers and an open grill. The restaurant now serves Tex-Mex specialities, such as Enchilada or chicken fajitas, as well as steaks. By the way, you won't have a problem finding a good steak at Disneyland Paris because all the meat is very good quality Angus beef from Aberdeen.

Starters cost from 20 to 47F and include chicken wings with barbeque sauce. Steaks are priced at 95 to 120F. Desserts cost 35–44F and include cheesecake and pecan pie. Wine and beer are available with your meal.

Fast-Food Restaurants:

Fuente del Oro
Only open at weekends
An attractively designed Mexican cantina which is now just a snack bar serving a strange combination of chilli (28F) and filled doughnuts (10F). If you want Tex-Mex food, you'll have to pay more and go to Silver Spur Steakhouse.

Cowboy Cookout Barbeque
Set menus 30F and 50F (25F children)
Closed on Mondays and Tuesdays
Recommended for families. Huge, barn-style restaurant, cosy on a cold day, with wagon wheels on the walls, wooden tables and chairs, and a small

stage where the Cowhand Band performs. Standard fast food, like burgers and chicken (8–28F), but great fun for kids.

Last Chance Café
Snack bar overlooking Thunder Mountain, between Silver Spur Steakhouse and Lucky Nugget Saloon. Serves sandwiches (18F) and light refreshments.

ADVENTURELAND

Table-Service Restaurants:

Blue Lagoon Restaurant
Star Rating *****
Set menus 140F, 175F or 260F (45F children)
Closed on Mondays and Tuesdays
Don't miss this one! This is the most imaginative of the Disney restaurants and well worth splashing out on. You will probably be tempted to eat here when you pass on the Pirates of the Caribbean ride. It's a wonderfully cool, tranquil place to come on a hot summer's evening.

This romantic underground restaurant has been designed in the Caribbean style, complete with white sand beach, bamboo furnishings and a terrace overlooking the water where the pirate boats glide by. A steel band plays in the evening.

The restaurant specialises in seafood, although curiously enough the most popular dish here is the steak! Starters cost from 35 to 55F and include prawn cocktail, seafood platter and a Caribbean salad. Main courses cost from 80 to 140F and include grilled fish, lobster, beef, fish wrapped in banana leaves and grilled sirloin. Desserts cost 30–45F and include crème brulée with coconut milk, banana cake with rum ice-cream and raisins and tropical fruits. Wines and beers are available with your meal.

Although this is the most romantic restaurant at Disneyland Paris and so ideal for dîner-à-deux, children will also enjoy the chance to watch the boats passing.

Fast-Food Restaurants:

Colonel Hathi's Pizza Outpost
Set menu 50F (25F children)
Closed on Wednesdays and Thursdays
It's sad to see that the old Explorer's Club restaurant has closed, but at least the beautiful building is still there, now serving pizzas and pasta fast-food style and renamed Colonel Hathi's.

Set up a junglefied path, main courses include four-cheese pizza (38F) smoked salmon pizza (40F), warm garlic rolls (10F) and tiramisu (20F) for dessert. Small pizzas (18F) are also available.

Pasta and pizza are also served at Pizzeria Bella Notte in Fantasyland.

Snacks:

Café de la Brousse
Only open at weekends
If you just want a bag of chips (10–15F) this hut by the water, opposite Adventure Isle, is where to come. They also sell filled doughnuts.

Captain Hook's Galley
Small snack bar served from the cannon bays of
Captain Hook's Pirate Ship.

FANTASYLAND

Table-Service Restaurants:

Auberge de Cendrillon
Star Rating ****
Set menus 140F, 175F or 260F (45F children)
Closed on Mondays and Tuesdays
Situated in the centre of Fantasyland with
Cinderella's carriage parked outside, this is the
restaurant that attracts the most attention at
Disneyland Paris – you can't miss it! Inside there
are candy-pink tablecloths, candles and wrought
iron chandeliers.

Starters cost 35–70F and include asparagus
in puff pastry with truffle butter, smoked salmon
or foie gras. Main courses cost from 97 to 130F
and include stuffed guinea fowl, duck drumsticks
and veal medallions. Desserts cost from 34 to
44F and include morello cherries and ice-cream,
Cinderella's Slipper and a Rhapsody in
Chocolate. Wine and beer are available with your
meal.

A la carte prices in this restaurant are fraction-
ally more than in the other table-service restaurants, so it's worth opting for one of the set menus.

In the summer you can eat outside on an attractive terrace where Cinderella's carriage is displayed.

Fast-Food Restaurants:

Pizzeria Bella Notte
Closed on Mondays and Tuesdays
This is a prime example of how beautifully designed the Disney fast-food restaurants are. When you first walk in, it looks like a table-service Italian restaurant with pitchers of grapes on the walls, wine barrels on the ceiling, Roman mosaic fountains and an open fire. It is actually run like a typical take-away pizza restaurant – you can carry your pizza off in a cardboard box.

There are plenty of tables inside and out at which you may sit and eat your meal. The menu includes spaghetti bolognese (28F) and a selection of pizzas (36–40F). Other dishes include lasagne (36F), garlic bread (10F) and tiramisu (20F).

Pizzas and pasta dishes also available at Colonel Hathi's in Adventureland.

Au Châlet de la Marionette
Set menus 30F or 50F (25F children)
Closed on Wednesdays and Thursdays
This is a good restaurant to come to on a cold, wet day – it's very warm and there's lots of space. Styled like a large alpine chalet, the menu comprises standard fast food such as hamburgers (8–17F), half a spit-roasted chicken (32F), chips (10–15F) and desserts such as fruit salad (12F) and doughnuts (10F).

Burgers and similar food are also available at Café Hyperion in Discoveryland.

Toad Hall Restaurant
Set menu 50F
Only open at weekends

Stop for fish and chips at Toadie's old baronial home, complete with Toad wallpaper, vaulted ceilings, leather chairs, draped velvet curtains, stained-glass windows and framed portraits of Wind in the Willow characters. Dishes from 15–25F.

Snacks:

March Hare Refreshments
Outdoor café serving punch, soft drinks and Unbirthday (chocolate and vanilla) cake.

Fantasia Gelati
Ice-cream parlour located next door to Pizzeria Bella Notte, which now sells much more reasonably prized soft ice-creams for 9F.

The Old Mill
Outdoor café serving frozen yoghurt ice-cream (14F), sandwiches (17F), fruit tarts (16F) and crisps (5F). Expect big queues on sunny days.

DISCOVERYLAND

Fast-Food Restaurants:

Café Hyperion
An enormous tiered, self-service restaurant, complete with tables and chairs, a high-tech interior, and painted in lime green and burnt orange. This is a good place to come on a cold, wet day. Young children will appreciate the chance to sit down, rest and watch some Disney cartoons on the giant screens. Teenagers will love the futuristic disco setting with muted disco music in background and

laser beams over the dance floor. The giant video screens show pop videos and there are also live brass bands. Do come here at least once for lunch as it's the chance to watch the superb Beauty and the Beast Show (see page 187 for review).

Fast food is now divided into two sections to help minimise the queues. At one counter you'll find burgers (9F for a cheeseburger), chips (10–15F) and chicken nuggets (25F). At the other you'll find sandwiches (17–18F) and salads (18F). Desserts include sundaes (9F), doughnuts (10F) and brownies (12F).

EATING AND DRINKING IN FESTIVAL DISNEY

The restaurants at Festival Disney are now franchised by the Flo restaurants company, although the theming has stayed the same since the park opened. Again, we have awarded the restaurants a star rating (* to *****), based on atmosphere, service, quality of food and value for money. Most of the restaurants also offer special set menus at reduced prices.

Despite their high prices, the Festival Disney restaurants get very busy, so it's best to book.

Annette's Diner
*Star Rating ****
Children always like this lively restaurant and the burgers are now much more affordable. It's a 1950s-style hamburger bar with a mint-and-peach colour scheme, formica tablecloths, plastic seats and a couple of cast members on roller skates. Standard burger and chips (39.50F) or chilli

(59.50F) are on offer. The kid's meal at 34.50F comprises a small hamburger, chips, drink and an ice-cream.

Fast-Food Restaurants:

Carnegie's Deli

New York-style café serving crunchy sandwiches in delicious French bread (17–29.50F) and croque monsieur (26.50F). Good place to grab a snack. Small restaurant with formica tables and food served in plastic basket trays, although many people queue for take-aways.

Key West Seafood

Star Rating *****

If you are going to splash out on a meal at Festival Disney, this is the most interesting and atmospheric of the restaurants, and it is ideal if you like seafood.

The decor is very attractive – a long oyster bar down one side of the room, giant models of fish hanging from the ceiling and pictures of sailing craft on the walls. There are two circular dining-rooms overlooking the water, as well as a narrow connecting room which can accommodate large groups of people on long tables.

Cast members are dressed in stripy t-shirts and white aprons. You are assigned a 'Captain' (ours was Captain Claus), rather than a waiter. The atmosphere is lively and raucous and children will enjoy banging the table with the crab mallet!

Starters include grilled stuffed mussels (42.50F) and Fisherman's Soup (39.50F). Main courses include seared salmon and fresh pasta (86.50F) and baked sole with spinach (89.50F). Desserts include crème brulée, lemon pie and almond cake. Wines are available from 89–142F (75cl).

Los Angeles Bar and Grill
Star Rating ****

Located at the Lake Buena Vista entrance to Festival Disney, this is a bright and attractive Californian restaurant with lots of light-coloured wood and a relaxed, informal atmosphere.

Popular with families, it offers a more varied venue than any of the other Festival Disney restaurants. Starters cost from 24.50 to 39.50F and include tomato and mozzarella salad, soup, quiche and salads. Main courses include pizzas (46.50–59.50F), pasta dishes (59.50–79.50F), salmon, steak and sliced lamb with garlic butter dishes (79.50–94.50F). Desserts range from 24.50–39.50F and offer apple tart, chocolate cake and tiramisu. Children's menu 45F. Wines can be bought for 89–142F (75cl) and cocktails from 40–55F.

The Steakhouse
Star Rating ***

This would have a higher rating if the prices were only a little lower. It's a smart steakhouse, but it charges outrageous prices for the albeit beautifully tender meat which it serves. Starters include a warm goat's cheese salad (42.50F) and main courses range from 104.5–154.50F. Desserts include ice-cream (28.50F) and profiterolles (44.50F).

The restaurant has tables inside and outside.

FESTIVAL DISNEY BARS

Sports Bar

This is a large saloon bar with lifesize models of American sports heros, which usually caters to a lively, young crowd. There are tables inside and out. Also serves food such as fish and chips (35F) and pizza (25F). Children's menu offers a hot dog, chips, drink and a surprise for 28F. Beers cost from 20F; a glass of wine, 20F; and cocktails from 35F. Cokes cost 12F.

Billy Bob's Bar

Country and western bar with live music every evening. Cocktails 45–49F. Food includes spare ribs (39F), chilli (39F) and chicken wings (39F).

Rock 'n' Roll America

Large 1960s-style bar serving beers (30F for a Kronenbourg), spirits (35F) and cocktails (35–55F). Sandwiches (25F), chilli (39F) and chicken and chips with salad (42F) are also served.

HOTEL RESTAURANTS

All the hotels have themed restaurants, and are licensed to serve alcohol. Prices in these are not usually any higher than in the restaurants in Festival Disney. Indeed, some of the hotel restaurants, such as the Chuck Wagon Café, are actually very good value.

Below is a brief round-up of hotel restaurants, highlighting the particularly good ones.

Hotel Disneyland

Café Fantasia: Fun, Disney themed café serving sandwiches and ice-creams.

Inventions: Recommended. Good restaurant for buffet meals of regional American cuisine, breakfast, lunch and dinner.

California Grill: Casual, elegant dining with Californian cuisine.

Hotel New York

Parkside Diner: New York-style diner. Good for breakfast and for family suppers (burgers, pizzas, club sandwiches, steaks and salads).

Newport Bay Club

Cape Cod: Recommended. Informal restaurant – good for pastas, pizzas and seafood. (Recently enlarged.)

The Yacht Club: Specialises in shellfish. Try their New England Clambake (steamed clams, potatoes, sausages, chicken, lobster and corn on the cob). (Recently enlarged.)

Sequoia Lodge

Beaver Creek Tavern: Disappointing family restaurant with little atmosphere and tasteless food.

Hunter's Grill: Rotisserie specialising in marinated meats served from skewers at your table.

Hotel Cheyenne

Chuck Wagon Café: Recommended. Self-service restaurant styled like a Western town with nine different wagons selling speciality dishes. Good value for families. All the food is served cowboy style on pewter plates and bowls, and there's lots of space for the kids to run around.

Hotel Santa Fe

La Cantina: Friendly self-service restaurant specialising in Tex-Mex dishes such as black bean soup and chilli con carne. Reasonably priced.

Camp Davy Crockett

Crockett's Tavern: Recommended. Small, clean self-service restaurant serving excellent hamburgers and other family fare, freshly cooked on a big grill in front of you. The large salad bar is also a treat. Reasonably priced.

CHAPTER EIGHT

THE UNOFFICIAL
SHOPPING GUIDE

*This chapter is intended for shopaholics who really
want to savour the shopping at Disneyland Paris.
It is also for people who hate shopping but want to
know where the best things are, so that they can
whizz round buying souvenirs and presents as
quickly as possible.*

*All the shops at Disneyland Paris – in the theme
park, in the hotels and in Festival Disney – are
reviewed, gift items are recommended and the best
shops are highlighted. For details about shopping
in Paris, see page 254.*

Not a Place for Bargains!

Disneyland Paris is certainly not a place to come shopping for bargains. One father from Wimbledon, while holidaying with his two young sons, said he spent £900 on souvenirs (mostly t-shirts!) for ten of his friends. However, there are now many more inexpensive souvenirs to buy than when the park first opened. In this chapter, we guide you round the best shops and suggest the better value presents and goods you can buy.

Most of the shops stock overpriced Disney memorabilia. Disney and Mickey Mouse motifs are to be found on absolutely everything from golf clubs to lollipops. If you know where to look, however, you will also find some very high-quality goods, and famous brand names such as Benetton, Levi's, Lalique, Osh Kosh and Crabtree & Evelyn.

There is no point in bargain hunting in Disneyland Paris as prices are standardised and you will pay the same for a Mickey hat, whichever shop you buy it in.

A Shopping Paradise for Children

All the shops at Disneyland Paris are themed, and goods are beautifully displayed – a big temptation for children and a potential nightmare for their parents! By following the guidelines of this chapter you will see which shops are really worth visiting so that you can promise to take the children to specific ones, rather than dashing into all of them and then having to deal with screaming tantrums when they want to leave with half the stock!

The Pleasures of Hassle-free Shopping

One of the nice aspects of shopping in Disneyland

Paris is that you are under no pressure to buy and cast members never disturb you from browsing, even in the more expensive shops.

Best Times to Shop

If you are only there for a day, you will probably want to leave the shopping until the end of it. The shops do get very busy at about 6 p.m., so you may want to wait until a bit later – just before the park closes. On longer stays, a good time to shop is first thing in the morning as the shops are usually quiet then. There are coin-operated lockers where you can leave small purchases underneath Main Street, USA, station. Bulkier items can be checked in with a cast member at Guest Storage.

Credit Cards and Travellers' Cheques

You can pay by American Express, Eurocard, Master Card,Visa or Carte Bleue at nearly all the Disneyland Paris shops.

At the Disney hotels and at Festival Disney, you can pay by travellers' cheques, but they are not accepted in the theme park.

TOP OF THE SHOPS

Here is our personal selection of the best and most interesting shops in Disneyland Paris:

Le Coffre du Capitaine (Adventureland) – Presents with a pirates theme.

Storybook Store (Main Street, USA) – Books and audio cassettes of favourite Disney stories available in several European languages.

167

Tobias Norton (Frontierland) – High quality Wild West souvenirs.

Star Traders (Discoveryland) – Presents with a *Star Wars* theme.

La Chaumière des Sept Nains (Fantasyland) – The place to come for children's Disney fancy-dress outfits.

La Boutique du Château (Fantasyland) – Specialist Christmas shop with trees and decorations.

Harrington's (Main Street, USA) – Elegant shop for fine china, porcelain, Lalique glass and quality gifts.

Dapper Dan's Hair Cuts (Main Street, USA) – A chance to have an old-time shave and haircut.

Disney Clothiers Ltd (Main Street, USA) – Good quality Disney clothing in a beautifully designed shop.

Adventureland Bazaar (Adventureland) – Fun and atmospheric place to browse.

La Confiserie des Trois Fées (Fantasyland) – If your children insist on going into one of the sweet shops, take them to this delightful little shop where there are floating fairies in the chimney breast.

Buffalo Trading Company (Festival Disney) – Presents with a Wild West theme.

SHOP REVIEWS

Like the rides and attractions, the shops have been graded (* to *****) and reviewed land by land, in a clockwise direction, starting in Main Street, USA.

MAIN STREET, USA

Main Street, USA, is a shopaholics paradise, although many of the shops stock similar merchandise. There are two big shopping arcades, and they are good places to browse if the weather is bad.

The quietest time to shop in Main Street, USA, is in the morning; the busiest, at the end of the day.

Plaza West Boutique
Star Rating *

A very ordinary Disney shop, this sells general merchandise and souvenirs. Most of the goods that you find here, you will also find elsewhere. If it looks like it is going to rain, it would be a good idea to buy your Mickey poncho now, before you start touring the park. Other goods include Mickey ears, Donald Duck caps, souvenir mugs and sunglasses.

Storybook Store
Star Rating ****

Don't be fooled by the dusty facsimile books in the window of this shop as inside it is full of Disney books and music cassettes. You should definitely find your favourite story here, with editions in several languages. Despite being advertised as a 'books and records' store, there are no records, only cassettes and compact discs. While you are browsing through the books, look up above at the Disney characters unloading dusty tomes from the shelves. Tigger is waiting at a counter at the exit to stamp your purchase.

Merchandise includes Ladybird books, Disney crayons, Lion King stickers and stamps, and Disney Souvenir Cassettes.

Liberty Arcade (Emporium)
*Star Rating ****
This is an excellent spot to come to if it rains. As well as going to the shops, you can wander through the arcade to look at the Statue of Liberty Tableau and find out more about the French-American alliance in making Lady Liberty a symbol of freedom to the world.

The arcade houses the Emporium, a turn-of-the-century department store with a beautiful, domed stained-glass ceiling. In the store you will find some useful items such as a disposable flash camera with film – in case you have forgotten your camera – and all sorts of clothing and presents for the whole family from baby to granny. Goods include quilted 101 Dalmatian romper suits, Mickey rucksacks, Minnie Mouse nightshirts, Aladdin teapots, Alice dresses, Mickey chocolates, fun ties and jewellery, and Disneyland Paris car stickers.

As you walk through the department store you come to *The Toy Chest* which stocks a huge range of cuddly toys and games. Some of these, such as Little Mermaid rubber stamps set (70F) are very overpriced. *Blixby Brothers* is also part of the

Emporium. The merchandise here is centred on the Lion King.

Dapper Dan's Hair Cuts
*Star Rating ****

If you rushed out of bed and forgot to shave, you can stop off at this corner shop for an old-fashioned shave (90F) or a haircut (90F, or 70F for children). The shop also sells shaving mugs and nostalgic shaving items.

Glass Fantasies
*Star Rating ***

Here you can watch a glass-blower creating knitted glass fantasies such as Sleeping Beauty's Castle, a mini Mickey Mouse and an amazingly ornate Cinderella's carriage.

Disney and Company
*Star Rating ***

The most original part about this shop is the fairground-theme decor with its distorted mirrors and colourful hot-air balloon. The goods on sale are similar to what you find in other shops, that is, Mickey ponchos and cuddly toys. Mickey and Minnie Breakfast sets are fun for junior members of the family.

Discovery Arcade
This is located on the opposite side of Main Street to Liberty Arcade and is inspired by European inventors/writers Jules Verne and H.G. Wells. It features a host of curious inventions dating from the Industrial Revolution of the 1880s. If you are in need of shelter you can walk through the arcade

and look at display cabinets of olde-worlde household items, toys and clothing. You can also sit in the arcade with a coffee or ice-cream bought from the arcade side of the Main Street cafés.

Harrington's Fine China and Porcelains
Star Rating *****
If you enter this shop from the arcade, you may think that all it sells is cheap, china Disney souvenirs. The best merchandise is on the Main Street side of this elegant shop, with its stained-glass-domed ceilings and ornate chandeliers and gilt pillars. The prices of some of the goods may knock you back – 14,000F for a porcelain tableau of Pinocchio and 3,500F for a Mickey puppet! More reasonable gifts are available. Stocks Lladro, Royal Albert bone china, Crummels hand-painted English enamels and Lalique glass.

Main Street Motors
Star Rating ***
Small shop selling automobile memorabilia. This is also where you can have an old-time portrait photo taken on a vintage car (from 125F).

Disney Clothiers Ltd
Star Rating *****
The place to come for quality Disney clothing, such as embroidered Goofy sweatshirts 250F, men's shirts with Mickey motif 250F, or silk ties 200F. The decor is elegant – styled like an old drawing-room with thick, rich carpet, piano and tailor's dummy. Clothing for all ages including fancy-dress outfits for children (Alice robes, Snow White dresses, etc).

172

Boardwalk Candy Palace
Star Rating ***

Atlantic City sweet palace with marble floor and pretty decor. The place to buy giant lollies, Disney confectionery, chocolate and homemade creamy butter fudge. You can even watch the fudge being made on the premises.

Town Square Photography
Star Rating *

Old-fashioned photographic shop selling films, cameras and accessories. Don't make the mistake of getting your photos developed here as it is very overpriced. A 36-picture film would cost 168.20F to develop in two hours! Cameras can be rented for 50F per day (plus 500F deposit), or you can buy a Kodak Fun Flash 35mm camera and film for 95F. Video cameras can be rented for 300F per day (plus 5,000F deposit). It also sells Disney theme music and videos.

Ribbons and Bows Hat Shop
Star Rating **

Pretty Victorian milliner's shop with candy pink wallpaper and pink velvet drapes. Disappointingly there are no old-fashioned ribbons for sale, only touristy hats.

FRONTIERLAND

Thunder Mesa Mercantile Building
Star Rating *****

Three high-quality, Wild West shops housed under one roof. *Tobias Norton & Sons* stocks leather items, cowboy hats and gifts such as toy pistols, neckerchief and silver cactus brooches. *Bonanza Outfitters* sells Wild West clothing such as suede waistcoats, Wild West t-shirts, buffalo button covers and bootlace ties. It also sells Indian-style goods such as headbands (fun for the kids) and chief head-dresses. *Eureka Mining Supplies* sells Wild West toys (gun and holster sets), model cowboys, Davy Crockett hats and food gifts such as peanut-butter nuggets, popcorn and root beer.

Pueblo Trading Post
Star Rating **
Small shop selling Winnie the Pooh character clothing, accessories, gift items and books, displayed in an American South-western atmosphere.

Woodcarver's Workshop
Star Rating **
Traditional Indian carvings of animals and Red Indian heads. Wood-working demonstrations.

ADVENTURELAND

Indiana Jones Adventure Outpost
Star Rating ***
Pagoda-style thatched cabin, evoking the style of the *Indiana Jones* movie, and selling goods such as Indiana Jones back-packs, rubber snakes and bush hats.

Adventureland Bazaar
Star Rating *****
This exotic bazaar is fun to browse in, although, if you have ever shopped in these eastern countries,

prices in Disneyland Paris's bazaar will seem very high and there is no chance of bartering! The atmosphere, however, is great, with lots of exotic murals, fountains and carved archways as well as impressive props, such as the dusty Land Rover parked outside *Le Girafe Curieuse* (stocks safari clothing and accessories). *Le Chant des Tam-Tams* sells wicker baskets, pottery and drums. *Les Trésors de Schéhérazade* has an Arabian feel to it with a giant camel walk-through and a selection of ornate clothing and exotic jewellery. *La Reine des Serpents* sells photographic books of eastern countries such as Morocco, Egypt and Turkey, pretty perfume bottles, ceramic bowls and unusual gifts for children, such as pharaoh masks. L'Echoppe d'Aladdin is good for ethnic jewellery.

Le Coffre du Capitaine
Star Rating *****
After riding on the Pirates of the Caribbean, you can stop off here to buy your pirate's hat and pistol. This is a fun shop that stocks all sorts of pirate novelties including stuffed parrots, wooden globes, toy telescopes, rubber daggers and Captain's (plastic) hook.

FANTASYLAND

La Boutique du Château
Star Rating ****
Specialist Christmas shop with trees and decorations, Christmas cards, wrapping paper and advent calendars. Goods include knitted stockings, Snow White and the Seven Dwarfs Tree Set, Victorian-style Christmas decorations and potpourri.

Merlin L'Enchanteur
Star Rating **
Gift shop selling German glass-blown goods, pottery dragons, tapestries, William Morris writing paper and range of pewter mugs and plates.

La Confiserie des Trois Fées
Star Rating ****
Pretty little sweet shop with range of Disneyfied confectionery, teddy bear biscuits and giant lollies. Look out for the floating fairies in the chimney breast!

La Chaumière des Sept Nains
Star Rating *****
Styled like a castle with suits of armour, this is the best place to buy Disney outfits for the kids, as Snow White dresses, Minnie dresses and Alice robes are all at 295F. Also in stock is Sleeping Beauty's tiara and Tinkerbell's dress and wand. Other goods include, baby Minnie Mouse slippers, Pooh Bear rucksacks, Mickey's pyjama case and Disney sun specs. Also sells cuddly toys and baby clothes.

Sir Mickey's
Star Rating ***
This shop is divided into two sections: *La Menagerie du Royaume* stocks cuddly toys, ceramics and glassware; while *Le Brave Petit Tailleur* sells Disney clothing (such as Mickey baseball caps).

La Bottega di Geppetto
Star Rating ***

A woodcarver's shop selling standard Disney goods such as children's clothing and cuddly toys. Also sells a few wooden dolls, puppets and music boxes.

DISCOVERYLAND

Constellations
Star Rating *
On central display in this shop is Mickey in his flying machine. Goods comprise standard Disney gifts and cuddly toys.

Star Traders
Star Rating *****
Fun futuristic-style shop selling Star Tours clothing, rubber *Star Wars* masks and laser guns.

FESTIVAL DISNEY

There are more themed boutiques at Festival Disney:

Bureau de Poste
Post Office, telephones and bureau to change money.

The Disney Store
Star Rating ***
Big store selling standard Disney merchandise such as mugs, toys, t-shirts, posters and books. Good for baby and children's clothes.

Team Mickey
Star Rating **

The Disneyland Paris or Mickey motif is on every imaginable sporting good from tennis rackets to golf clubs. Sells golfing, tennis, baseball, American football and fitness merchandise.

Hollywood Pictures
Star Rating *****
Now known as the *Boutique Lion King* with a wide variety of goods with this theme, plus other specialist goods such as Tintin and Aladdin. This shop leads into *Mattel World of Toys* where you can buy a huge array of dolls and model Disney characters including Mary Poppins, Peter Pan, Captain Hook, Beauty and the Beast and Sleeping Beauty. Also sells Barbie dolls, toy cars and Horror Pets.

Buffalo Trading Company
Star Rating *****
The Wild West clothing and goods sold here include Frontierland t-shirts, jewellery, Stetsons, Davy Crockett hats and cowboy boots.

DISNEY HOTELS

You will also find shops in the hotels. These sell the usual Disney merchandise at the same price as in the theme park, as well as those designer clothes and gifts which fit in with the particular theme of the hotel.

Disneyland Hotel: Galerie Mickey
Star Rating **
Victorian-style shop selling Disney merchandise and designer clothes by Lacoste, Théorème, Cacharel and Diapositive.

Hotel New York: Stock Exchange
Star Rating ****
The best hotel shop because, apart from Disney memorabilia, it stocks high-quality goods such as leather jackets, glitzy New York-style bags and t-shirts that teenagers will particularly like, plus stripy shirts for dad and bags and scarves for mum.

Newport Bay Club: Bay Boutique
Star Rating ***
Clothing with a nautical theme: nautical books and gifts as well as designer clothes and Disney memorabilia.

Sequoia Lodge: North-West Passage
Star Rating ***
National Park theme gifts and Disney memorabilia.

Hotel Cheyenne: General Store
Star Rating **
Wild West theme goods and clothing as well as Disney memorabilia.

Hotel Santa Fe: Trading Post
Star Rating *
Small shop selling Disney memorabilia and cheap-looking New Mexico theme goods.

Camp Davy Crockett: Alamo Trading Post
Star Rating **
Big store in the camp village, selling Disney memorabilia plus food, drink and provisions for your cabin.

BEST BUYS

If you don't want to spend too much time shopping, the lists below should help direct you to some of the most interesting and best buys in the resort.

Suggested Gift List for Grown-ups:

Clothing

Winnie the Pooh embroidered waistcoat 349F (Disney Clothiers Ltd: Main Street, USA)

101 Dalmatian nightshirt and bed socks 195F (Emporium: Main Street, USA)

Goofy rugby shirt 157F (Emporium: Main Street, USA)

Disney boxer shorts 100F (Emporium: Main Street, USA)

Cowboy boots 750–1,300F (Tobias Norton: Frontierland)

Wild West t-shirts 175F (Bonanza Outfitters: Frontierland)

Silver Disneyland Paris jacket 250F (Star Traders: Discoveryland)

Tartan Mickey nightshirt 225F (Le Petit Tailleur: Fantasyland)

Books

The Art of Walt Disney 295F (Storybook Store: Main Street, USA)

Disneyland Paris souvenir book (paperback) 35F (Emporium: Main Street, USA)

Novelties

Winnie the Pooh music box 165F (Emporium: Main Street, USA)

Embroidered Lion King denim shirt 295F (Bixby Brothers: Main Street, USA)

Mickey belt-buckle 35F (Bonanza Outfitters: Frontierland)

Embroidered Advent calendar 165F (La Boutique du Château: Fantasyland)

Star Trek Deep Space Nine watch 150F (Star Traders: Discoveryland)

Team Mickey magic catch ball and glove (Team Mickey: Festival Disney)

Silly Gifts

Mickey Mouse ears 25F (Toy Chest: Main Street, USA)

Mickey Mouse slippers 125F (Emporium: Main Street, USA)

Rubber *Star Wars* warrior mask 242F (Star Traders: Discoveryland)

Goofy baseball cap 65F (Chaumière des Sept Nains: Fantasyland)

Wildly Extravagant

Porcelein Anniversary Tableau of Snow White and the Seven Dwarfs 28,000F (Harrington's: Main Street, USA)

Giant, cuddly Lion King 550F (Bixby Brothers: Main Street, USA)

Suggested Gift List for Children:

Accessories

Tartan Minnie bow for hair 25F (Ribbons and Bows, Main Street, USA)

Fez 55F (La Reine des Serpents: Main Street, USA)

Sleeping Beauty's tiara 35F (Boutique de
   Château: Fantasyland)
Snow White and the Seven Dwarfs pencil box 20F
   (Chaumière des Sept Nains: Fantasyland)

Toys
Mickey 3-D viewmaster 99F (Toy Chest: Main
   Street, USA)
Pack of rubber Seven Dwarfs 95F (Disney and
   Company: Main Street, USA)
Jasmine doll 189F (Constellations: Discoveryland)
8-sound laser gun 65F (Star Traders: Discovery-
   land)

Fancy Dress
Gun and holster set 75-125F (Eureka Mining
   Supplies: Frontierland)
Stetson 250-295F (Tobias Norton: Frontierland)
Racoon-fur hat 55F (Eureka Mining Supplies:
   Frontierland)
Alice robe 295F (La Chaumière des Sept Nains:
   Fantasyland)
Snow White dress 190F (Disney Clothiers Ltd:
   Main Street, USA)
Pirate's hat 60F (Le Coffre du Capitaine:
   Adventureland)
Toy telescope 20F (Le Coffre du Capitaine:
   Adventureland)
Captain's hook (plastic) 20F (Le Coffre du
   Capitaine: Adventureland)

Cute and Cuddly
Cuddly Dumbo 150F (Disney and Company: Main
   Street, USA)
Cuddly Dalmatian Pup 100F (Disney and
   Company: Main Street, USA)

Cuddly Dwarf (one of seven available) 129F (Toy Chest: Main Sreet, USA)

Cuddly Tigger 100F (Constellations: Discoveryland)

Best for Baby

Dumbo baby's bottle 36F (Petit Tailleur: Fantasyland)

Starter feeding set 95F (Toy Chest: Main Street, USA)

Toddler's feeding cup 75F (Sir Mickey's: Fantasyland)

Cuddly baby Mickey 99F (Toy Chest: Main Street, USA)

Fun for School

Seven Dwarfs eraser set 30F (Storybook Store: Main Street, USA)

Mickey rucksack 65F (Emporium: Main Street, USA)

Mickey pencil box 29F (Toy Chest: Main Street, USA)

Star Tours rucksack 75F (Star Traders: Discoveryland)

CHAPTER NINE

THE UNOFFICIAL ENTERTAINMENT GUIDE

There is certainly no shortage of entertainment at Disneyland Paris, and most of the best events are free and included in the price of your entrance ticket.

In this chapter we review the entertainment in the park and in Festival Disney, as well as highlighting the entertainment in the hotels.

ENTERTAINMENT IN THE PARK

There are all sorts of entertainment and shows inside the park. When you arrive, go to City Hall in Main Street and ask for a weekly entertainment programme (*programme des spectacles*) as this will give you the times of all the shows you want to see.

Following are reviews of the main events, graded (from * to *****) for their entertainment value.

The Disney Parade (La Parade Disney)
*Entertainment Rating *****
Cost: free

Great fun for all ages and always a big hit with young children who love to watch their favourite characters ride down Main Street, USA, on colourful floats, and accompanied by music taken from the films that made them famous.

Some of the best floats include Pinocchio with dancing puppets; the pirates dancing aboard Hook's ship; the Jungle Book characters; Little Mermaid blowing bubbles; and Roger Rabbit in his concertina cartoon car.

New for 1995 is the Lion King float, which is accompanied by music written by Tim Rice and performed by Elton John. Simba is surrounded by an entourage of furry and frightening friends including ghoulish hyenas and colourful beetles who glide around the base of the float on rollerblades.

In order to get a good viewing spot, get there about half an hour before the parade begins. If it is too crowded to sit on the kerbside, perch on the railing around Central Plaza, in front of Sleeping Beauty's castle. From here you will see the start of the Parade, before it advances down Main Street, USA. Remember to face away from the sun or you will have to squint.

The marching band heralds the start of the Parade.

Main Street Electrical Parade
*Entertainment Rating *****
Cost: free
Magical evening parade with over half a million twinkling lights. As with the Disney Parade, you need to get there about half an hour beforehand for a good viewing spot.

Some of the floats are really spectacular. Look out for Dumbo who showers himself with twinkly lights and the happy faces of the It's A Small World dolls. Big Ben brings up the rear.

Fantasia in the Sky
*Entertainment Rating *****
Cost: free
This superb fireworks display bursts into vibrant colour over the Magic Kingdom after the Electrical Parade. It is accompanied by music from the film *Fantasia*. A truly spectacular end to a day at Disneyland Paris.

C'est Magique
*Entertainment Rating *****
Cost: free
Excellent show on Fantasy Festival Stage with Disney characters miming along to boppy tunes. This fun, lively show is the ideal opportunity to

rest for half an hour and watch your favourite Disney characters join a troupe of energetic dancers.

Make sure you find a seat at least 15 minutes before the advertised starting time, or you'll have to stand at the back or sides.

Beauty and the Beast
(Café Hyperion: Discoveryland)
Entertainment Rating *****
Cost: free
Superb show with cast miming to the songs from the film *Beauty and the the Beast*. Beautifully staged featuring highlighted scenes. A great show to watch over lunch.

Lilly's Follies
(Lucky Nugget Saloon: Frontierland)
Entertainment Rating ****
If you want some lively entertainment with dinner, this show is ideal. The plot is rather corny, but the cancan dancers are colourful and the atmosphere is lively. Children will enjoy clapping along to the tunes and watching the pantomime-style chase scenes which run through the auditorium.

You don't have to pay to eat to watch this show but the 80F menu (40F children) is good value and makes it more of a special event (see Restaurant Guide page 152).

Minnie's Teatime
Entertainment Rating **
Not a show as such, but a chance to meet Minnie and other Disney characters at Central Plaza in front of Sleeping Beauty's Castle.

Street Entertainers
Entertainment Rating ***
Cost: free
Wherever you go in Disneyland Paris, there are street performers to entertain you and enhance the atmosphere of the themed land.

A NIGHT OUT IN FESTIVAL DISNEY

Festival Disney (the entertainment centre) has improved greatly since Disneyland Paris opened in 1992 and, although it is still not the most attractive of architectural designs, it has at last come alive with a street carnival atmosphere.

Like prices in the park, the prices in Festival Disney have also been greatly reduced and the restaurants (apart from the Steakhouse) are no longer ripoffs. The Never-Never-Land Club (a children's crèche) has been replaced by a video arcade and there are numerous slot-machines throughout Festival Disney to amuse the kids. The best entertainment at Festival Disney is Buffalo Bill's Wild West Show.

Festival Disney is also licensed so you can go there just for a drink. Following is a round-up of the entertainment on offer.

Hurricane's
Entertainment Rating **
Cost: 120F entrance (includes one free drink). Entrance free for hotel guests.
Smallish discotheque where young teenagers can drink giant turquoise cocktails and bop the night away to Madonna and other poppy tunes. Unpretentious holiday atmosphere at inflated prices. Cocktails cost 50–65F.

THE UNOFFICIAL ENTERTAINMENT GUIDE

Buffalo Bill's Wild West Show

Entertainment Rating *****
Cost: 325F (200F for the under-12s)

This is one of the best attractions at Disneyland Paris, so it is a shame that it is so expensive. Some tour operators include tickets in the package or look out for special half-price deals when you're there.

Lively Wild West show and dinner starring Annie Oakley, Buffalo Bill, 40 cowboys and Indians and more than 80 horses, buffalo and longhorn steer. The Red Indian scene is particularly spectacular with real buffalo being rounded up by the Indians. Great fun for all the family.

Entrance fee includes dinner (good quality and lots of it), raucous entertainment and a straw cowboy hat. You don't have to pay for children under three – they will enjoy the opportunity to bash their bowl with their spoon and will love the excitement of all the chases, although they are likely to get bored by the audience games and competitions. Babies may find the noise level disturbing.

There are two shows every night – at 6.30 p.m. and 9.30 p.m. You can make your reservation in person at Festival Disney, at City Hall (Main Street, USA) or by phoning 60 45 71 00.

Billy Bob's Country and Western Saloon

Entertainment Rating **
Live country and western music at the bar.

ENTERTAINMENT IN THE HOTELS

Character Breakfasts

Hotel Disneyland, Key West restaurant in Festival Disney and Plaza Gardens in Main Street, USA

Entertainment Rating **
Cost: 140F (105F for kids)
Buffet breakfast in the top-bracket hotels attended by Disney characters. Fun for little kids but don't expect a show or lots of characters. It's very laid back and during a typical hour-long breakfast you will probably only see four or five characters.

EVENINGS IN THE HOTELS

Each hotel offers live entertainment in their bars or restaurants.

Disneyland Hotel – jazz band at Main Street Lounge.

Hotel New York – don't miss the Manhattan Jazz Club which has had rave reviews from French critics – some even recommend that you go to Disneyland Paris just to see the jazz in this club! For further information tel: 60 45 73 00.

Sequoia Lodge – piano music in the Redwood Bar.

Newport Bay Club – piano music in Fisherman's Wharf bar.

Hotel Cheyenne – country and western music in the Red Garter Saloon.

Hotel Santa Fe – Mexican musicians in La Cantina restaurant and in Rio Grande Bar.

Camp Davy Crockett – storytelling and singing by the campfire in the village (summer only).

CHAPTER TEN

TAKING YOUNG CHILDREN TO DISNEYLAND PARIS

Disneyland Paris can be the most magical place on earth for children, but as with any holiday, there are potential problems of taking very young children there.

In this chapter we give you tips and advice on touring the park with young children, advise you on the suitability of rides and give you practical suggestions on how to make your stay more enjoyable.

DISNEYLAND PARIS FOR CHILDREN

Children of all ages will enjoy Disneyland Paris, although, in our opinion, it is best appreciated by children over seven years old. Several of the rides have height restrictions and others may be psychologically unsuitable for very young children.

Financially, it's tempting to take tiny tots to Disneyland Paris as there is no entrance charge to the park for children under three years old, and most companies and hotels don't charge for a child under two years old sleeping in a cot in your room.

Tiny tots are usually thrilled, but slightly dazzled by all the bright colours and activities in the park. Children of this age (and some older ones too) can be frightened by some of the costumed characters. Even if they've been looking forward to seeing Mickey Mouse and his friends, it can come as a shock to encounter the giant version of them. Many confident little children break into hysterics when they get up close to these characters – so do approach them slowly.

The cast members who play these characters are highly skilled in the way they approach young children and will back off at the slightest sign of apprehension from the little ones. However, if your child shows any signs of being nervous, do keep a watchful eye on them as the characters sometimes misjudge this and may come up from behind to tap a child on the shoulder.

The Parade is always a popular choice for children, although bear in mind that even sections of this can be scary, particularly the fire-breathing dragon.

There are now many more characters in the park than when it first opened so your children should be able to meet their favourites. On arrival, ask for an entertainment programme at City Hall. This will tell you of scheduled times to meet the characters, such as at Minnie's Teatime when Minnie and her friends gather outside the castle to mingle with the children.

Babies
Babies may not remember that they were ever taken to Disneyland Paris but that's not to say they won't enjoy it, and the park is certainly baby friendly. There are changing-tables in the toilets (both ladies and gents), high chairs in every restaurant and staff who smile – even when your baby throws his food all over their immaculately swept floor. There is also an excellent Babycare Centre where you can feed, rest and change your child or purchase jars of baby food. Pushchairs can be rented and parked in special areas when you go on rides.

Suitability of Rides
If you are going to Disneyland Paris with young children, do check the suitability of individual rides (see Chapter Six) as some of them are not so ideal for very young children. There are not many warnings at Disneyland Paris about which rides are suitable for very young children and which are not. Many of the seemingly tame rides, such as Snow White and the Seven Dwarfs and Adventures of Pinocchio, can be terrifying for an imaginative toddler, or even older child, as they focus on the scary scenes. You do see parents

taking little ones on more daring rides such as the Pirates of the Caribbean (a boat ride through pirate land with some stomach churning roller-coaster sections), but this is not advisable unless your child is very placid. (See Chapter Twelve for detailed guided tours for families with young children.)

Teenagers

We have not devised specific guided tours for teenagers as they are likely to want to do their own thing or follow an adult's tour. Following, are some suggestions as to which rides they may particularly enjoy.

Top Attractions for Teenagers

Space Mountain (Discoveryland)
Indiana Jones and the Temple of Peril (Adventure-
  land)
Star Tours (Discoveryland)
Astroport (Discoveryland)
Captain EO (Discoveryland)
Big Thunder Mountain Railroad (Frontierland)
Phantom Manor (Frontierland)
Pirates of the Caribbean (Adventureland)
Nautilus (Discoveryland)
The Electrical Parade (Main Street, USA)
Buffalo Bill's Wild West Show (Festival Disney)

Toddlers

Parents with very young children will probably find our guided tours too intense and may like to make their own selection based on the following suggestions.

Top Rides for Toddlers *(see page 83 for reviews)*
Disneyland Paris Railroad (Main Street, USA)
Main Street Vehicles (Main Street, USA)
It's a Small World! (Fantasyland)
Peter Pan's Flight (Fantasyland)
Casey Junior (Fantasyland)
Le Pays de Contes des Fées (Fantasyland)
Lancelot's Carousel (Fantasyland)
Mad Hatter's Teacups (Fantasyland)
Dumbo the Flying Elephant (Fantasyland)
Orbitron (Discoveryland)
Cottonwood Creek Ranch (Frontierland)
Le Passage Enchanté d'Aladdin (Adventureland)
Beauty and the Beast (Discoveryland)

Top Entertainment for Toddlers
C'est Magique (Fantasyland)
The Parade (Main Street, USA)
The Electrical Parade (Main Street, USA)
Character Breakfasts (Disneyland Hotel, Key West restaurant in Festival Disney or Plaza Gardens in Main Street, USA)

Top Rides for Four to Seven Year Olds
Peter Pan's Flight (Fantasyland)
Sleeping Beauty's Castle (Fantasyland)
Snow White and the Seven Dwarfs (Fantasyland)
Adventures of Pinocchio (Fantasyland)
Mad Hatter's Teacups (Fantasyland)
Casey Junior (Fantasyland)
Swiss Family Robinson Tree-House (Adventureland)
Orbitron (Discoveryland)
Pirates of the Caribbean (Adventureland)
Indian Canoes (Frontierland)

Les Pirouettes du Vieux Moulins (Fantasyland)
Adventure Isle (Adventureland)

Top Entertainment for Four to Seven Year Olds

Beauty and the Beast (Videopolis: Discoveryland)
C'est Magique (Fantasyland)
The Parade (Main Street, USA)
The Electrical Parade (Main Street, USA)
Character Breakfasts (Disneyland Hotel, Key West restaurant in Festival Disney or Plaza Gardens in Main Street, USA)
Buffalo Bill's Wild West Show (Festival Disney)

Great for Grandparents!

Grandparents will find plenty of things to do and see – although they may, of course, be restricted with a toddler or two in tow. The park is not as big as it looks on the map but, if your feet get tired, you can always catch the train or one of the other vehicles down Main Street. Remember, feel free to sit down at any of the restaurant cafés, even if you are not eating or drinking.

Disneyland Paris Railroad (Main Street, USA)
Nautilus (Discoveryland)
Phantom Manor (Frontierland)
Pirates of the Caribbean (Adventureland)
Sleeping Beauty's Castle (Fantasyland)
Peter Pan's Flight (Fantasyland)
It's a Small World! (Fantasyland)
Le Visionarium (Discoveryland)
Le Pays du Contes des Fées (Fantasyland)
Beauty and the Beast (Discoveryland)
The Disney Parade (Main Street, USA)
The Electrical Parade (Main Street, USA)

GENERAL TIPS

There is a lot of walking to do at Disneyland Paris and children under three years old will certainly need a pushchair. If you don't bring your own, you may hire one for 30F at Town Terrace Square, Main Street, USA.

There is nothing more frightening for a young child than getting lost, and this could easily happen on a busy day at the park. Reins or a wrist strap are a good idea for roving toddlers. Children who are old enough to understand should be shown where the Lost Children Office is located (adjacent to Plaza Gardens Restaurant), in case you should get parted.

If you and your partner are touring the park with more than one child, you may decide to divide the children so that you can each take them on the rides most suitable for their age group. If so, do arrange a firm time and meeting place as otherwise the chances are that you won't bump into each other for the rest of the day. It's a good idea to choose a restaurant at which to meet, but allow at least half an hour's leeway in case one of you is held up with queues, or by junior insisting on doing the ride again. Messages for each other can also be left and picked up at City Hall. Café Hyperion in Discoveryland is a good place to meet in bad weather as it's a huge, tiered, undercover restaurant with cartoon shows and the Beauty and the Beast Show to amuse little ones while you wait.

Disneyland Paris can be very tiring for adults and quite overwhelming for young children. If you are staying in one of the hotels, take advantage of the opportunity to take your child back for a nap at lunchtime. This is particularly advantageous in summer as the park stays open late at night and a child who has been refreshed from a nap is far more able to cope with a longer day. From this point of view, the best hotel for families with young children is the, albeit expensive, Disneyland Hotel, since it's right next to the park.

For further information on good hotels for families see Chapter Four (Where to Stay), and for restaurants see Chapter Seven (The Unofficial Restaurant Guide).

CHAPTER ELEVEN

COPING WITH THE RAIN

Disneyland Paris does face climate and weather problems which aren't encountered in the American parks. In this chapter we give you guidelines on what to do and where to go when there's a downpour.

DISNEYLAND PARIS IN THE RAIN

Disney's magic can quickly wash away during a downpour. When checking in at your hotel, it's advisable to have a brolly in the car to make unloading more comfortable. The carparks are huge, so you may have a long walk back to the hotel when you've finally parked your car.

The hotels all have shuttle buses which are supposed to transport you to the park. In reality, they drop you outside the train station which means a further 5–10 minute walk, with no protection from the elements, before you reach the turnstiles. People coming in for the day by car or train face the same problems.

You really should take waterproof clothing to Disneyland Paris – whatever time of year you are going. If you do get caught short, you can buy plastic Mickey Mouse ponchos and umbrellas in the hotel shops, in Festival Disney and in the park itself.

Following are the best attractions to do in the rain.

MAIN STREET, USA

Disneyland Paris Railroad – the sides are open, however, so if the weather is very bad you won't get full protection!

Liberty Arcade – there are exhibits of the making of Lady Liberty as well as shops to explore.

Discovery Arcade – exhibits of inventions as well as housing shops and cafés.

FRONTIERLAND

Phantom Manor – house of spooks with most of the queueing under cover.

Thunder Mesa Mercantile Building – contains three shops selling high-quality Wild West clothing and gifts.

ADVENTURELAND
Pirates of the Caribbean – indoor boat ride.
Le Passage Enchanté d'Aladdin – browse through Aladdin's cave.
Adventureland Bazaar – series of interconnecting shops. Unfortunately, these are still a little cold and damp on particularly bad days. Only come here for shelter, if you get caught in this area.

FANTASYLAND
Sleeping Beauty's Castle
Snow White and the Seven Dwarfs
Pinocchio's Adventures
Peter Pan's Flight – but if the queues are very big you will have to wait in the rain.
Mad Hatter's Teacups
Fantasy Festival Stage – excellent show called C'est Magique.
It's A Small World!

DISCOVERYLAND
Le Visionarium – 3-D film. Big queues may mean a short wait in the rain.
Space Mountain – part of the queuing may be outside, but it's such an exciting ride that it will lift your spirits.
Nautilus – an undersea vessel is the best place to stay dry!
Star Tours – most of the queuing area is indoors.
Astroport – in the Star Tours buildings. Futuristic interactive games to play on.
Star Traders – interesting shop to browse in.

BEST PLACES TO EAT ON A WET DAY

Videopolis
Discoveryland
A great place to come in the rain. Choice of burgers, sandwiches or salads at Café Hyperion. Children can watch cartoons and the superb Beauty and the Beast Show.

Victoria's Homestyle Cooking
Main Street, USA
Nice and warm on a cold wet day. Serves similar snacks to those you might buy from a food cart.

Cable-Car Bake Shop
Main Street, USA
Warm, comfortable place to stop for tea and cakes on a wet afternoon.

Plaza Gardens Restaurant
Main Street, USA
Elegant self-service restaurant with live jazz at lunchtimes. A good place to escape from the rain.

Au Châlet de la Marionette
Fantasyland
Large, warm, fast-food restaurant near to those indoor children's rides, such as Peter Pan, Pinocchio and Snow White.

Cowboy Cookout Barbeque
Frontierland
Eat in this large, fast-food restaurant and warm yourself up by dancing to their lively country band.

Lucky Nugget Saloon
Frontierland
Relatively cheap food – 80F set menu (40F children) – and there's a show to watch, too.

Table-Service Restaurants
Treat yourself to a long lunch at *Auberge du Cendrillon* (Fantasyland), *Walt's* (Main Street, USA) or the *Silver Spur Steakhouse* (Frontierland). Don't go to the *Blue Lagoon* (Adventureland) when it's raining, as it feels cold and damp.

CHAPTER TWELVE

THE UNOFFICIAL GUIDED TOURS

As you can see from earlier chapters, there is much to see and do in Disneyland Paris. In this chapter we show you how to make the most of your stay by avoiding the worst of the queues, but still seeing all the best attractions, in a set amount of time.

We have included carefully detailed tours both for adults and for families with young children (4–7 year olds). If you only have a day, follow our Whirlwind Tours. If you stay longer, follow our Two-Day Tours. Also see Chapter Ten for tips on touring the park with children and to discover the best rides for children and babies.

Thrill-seeking teenagers can follow the adult tours or they may like to dash off at their own pace to do the most thrilling rides and attractions that we recommend for them.

Please check times of parades and shows at City Hall (Main Street, USA) as these vary throughout the season.

For budding David Baileys, we have also included a Photographic Tour, highlighting the best vantage points in the park.

THE WHIRLWIND TOUR FOR ADULTS

This has been specially designed to enable you to see and do all the best rides and attractions in one day, with minimal queuing.

8.45 a.m. Arrive at the gates, and buy your ticket.

8.55 a.m. Walk up Main Street, USA, and then, at 9 a.m., walk quickly through the fountain area of Plaza Gardens into Discoveryland. Go straight to **Space Mountain**, the latest Disney attraction, which makes you feel as though you've been launched into space.

9.30 a.m. Walk across to **Star Tours**, another very popular attraction, where queues quickly build up later in the day. This gives you a simulated six-minute trip into space in a *Star Wars*-type adventure setting.

9.45 a.m. Dash back across Plaza Gardens and into Frontierland for **Big Thunder Mountain Railroad**. At this time of the morning the queues should not be too bad and you should be able to board the runaway mining train in 20–30 minutes (later in the day the queues are horrendous). This is one of the best thrill rides in Disneyland Paris – don't miss it!

10.15 a.m. Don't linger! You've still got to do one more major thrill ride before the queues build up. So, walk over to **Indiana Jones and the Temple of Peril** for another runaway train experience, this time with a 360-degree loop!

11 a.m. Give yourself a chance to catch your breath after a hectic couple of hours! Take a leisurely walk through Adventureland and soak in the exotic atmosphere. Walk over the precarious plank bridges to explore Adventure Isle and then stop for a coffee at **Captain Hook's Galley** before climbing the **Swiss Family Robinson Tree-House**. The 90-foot tree is a prime example of Disney imagineering – it's entirely man-made, from its roots to its leaves, and all the tree-house rooms are packed with detail.

11.45 a.m. Now's the time to book a dinner table for tonight (for around 7.30 p.m.). The most atmospheric Disney restaurant, the **Blue Lagoon**, is here in Adventureland. This is a subterranean restaurant where you can sit in a tropical moonlit setting and watch the boats from the **Pirates of the Caribbean** glide by.

noon. Don't miss trying the **Pirates of the Caribbean** ride as this is a superbly imaginative 12-minute indoor boat ride through pirate-invaded territory with some wonderfully hairy moments when your boat has to escape from cannonfire. Great fun!

12.45 p.m. Leave Adventureland through the **Bazaar** (stop to shop if you have time and money). Head for the stunningly ornate **Sleeping Beauty's Castle** and see the wonderfully authentic dragon in the dungeon and the Disney tapestries and stained-glass windows in the gallery upstairs.

1 p.m. You are in a good position here to choose where you want to have lunch. Hot-dog fans can cross over to **Casey's Corner** (Main Street, USA); hot snacks like baked potatoes can be bought from **Victoria's Homestyle Cooking** on the opposite side of Main Street, USA. Or, you could go into Fantasyland and have fish and chips at **Toad Hall**; a burger at **Châlet de la Marionette**; or some pasta at **Pizzeria Bella Notte** (located on the other side of Fantasyland). If it's cold or raining and you want a long break, go to **Café Hyperion** in Discoveryland. There you can have a quick lunch and then take your seat for the superb **Beauty and the Beast Show** (1.30 p.m.).

2 p.m. Time to look round Fantasyland and see how the queues are building up! For a bit of a giggle, you may want a quick ride on the lavishly painted horses of **Le Carousel de Lancelot** (Lancelot's Roundabout) or take to the skies with **Dumbo the Flying Elephant** (both designed with the under-sevens in mind). The queues are never too bad for the **Mad Hatter's Teacups**, a typical fairground ride which whirls you round and round in giant cups. Alternatively, if it's sunny, you can wander round **Alice's Curious Labyrinth**, a complex maze leading to the **Queen of Hearts' Castle**. The best ride in Fantasyland is **Peter Pan** but now, in the middle of the day, the queues are usually too big, so wait to do this one in the evening.

The most famous Disney ride of all is **It's A Small World!**, a leisurely, indoor boat ride through a world of beautifully costumed singing and dancing dolls. A bit twee, but fun.

207

2.50 p.m. Take your place at Central Plaza for the 3 p.m. **Parade** of Disney characters.

3.30 p.m. Stop for tea and cakes at the **Cable-Car Bake Shop**, or enjoy an ice-cream at **Gibson Girl's Ice-Cream Parlour**. Then walk off the calories by returning to Frontierland and **Phantom Manor**. The latter is one of the most imaginative rides at Disneyland Paris – a chilling journey round the haunted house in a swivelling carriage – lots of fun!

4.30 p.m. Spend a little while wandering around Frontierland where there is always plenty to watch, such as the cowboy shoot-outs, the **Molly Brown Steamboat** and the screaming crowds on **Thunder Mountain**.

5 p.m. Jump on the **Disneyland Railroad** at Frontierland Station and travel round to Discoveryland.

5.15 p.m. Return to Discoveryland to watch **Le Visionarium**, a 360-degree vision film about time-travel, starring Jeremy Irons and Gerard Depardieu.

5.45 p.m. Head for **Captain EO** – a 3-D film, starring a crew of cuddly animals, a robot, and Michael Jackson as funky Captain EO. Afterwards, take to the skies in **Orbitron**, a flying machine that is low on thrills but beautifully designed. Alternatively, drive round **Autopia** in an open-topped racing car – this ride is rather tame and only really fun for people who haven't yet passed their driving test.

6.30 p.m. Don't miss **Nautilus** and the chance to explore Captain Nemo's undersea vessel.

7 p.m. Cut back through **Sleeping Beauty's Castle** and into the bazaar that leads into Adventureland. Walk over to **Blue Lagoon** for your 7.30 p.m. dinner.

9 p.m. Time for a quick after-dinner stroll. Disneyland Paris is even more magical in the dark. Particularly spectacular are Adventureland, with its flaming torches and exotic bazaar, and Main Street, USA, with all its intricately designed buildings lit up.

9.20 p.m. Find a good spot on Main Street to watch the **Electrical Parade**. (This only occurs at weekends and Bank Holidays.)

10 p.m. Dash back to Fantasyland to do **Peter Pan's Flight**. Queues are normally horrendous for this kiddies' favourite, but most of them will have gone home by this time. Alternatively, have another ride on your favourite thrill ride (**Space Mountain**, **Thunder Mountain Railroad** or **Indiana Jones and the Temple of Peril**).

THE TWO-DAY TOUR FOR ADULTS

With two days to spend, adults can enjoy a more leisurely tour of the attractions – with time to discover some of Disneyland Paris's Entertainment.

Day One

8.45 a.m. Arrive at the gates, and buy a two-day ticket.

8.55 a.m. Walk up Main Street, USA, to queue to the right of the barrier leading into Central Plaza.

9 a.m. Walk quickly through the fountain area of Plaza Gardens into Discoveryland, and go straight to **Space Mountain**, the latest Disney attraction, which catapults you into space in a rocket.

9.30 a.m. Walk across to **Star Tours**, another very popular attraction, where queues quickly build up later in the day. This gives you a simulated six-minute trip into space in a *Star Wars*-type adventure setting.

10 a.m. Walk round **Nautilus** to explore the undersea vessel of Captain Nemo.

10.20 a.m. Watch **Le Visionarium**, a 360-degree vision film about time-travel, starring Jeremy Irons and Gerard Depardieu.

11 a.m. Get a breath of fresh air by taking to the skies in **Orbitron**.

11.15 a.m. Time for another movie – this time the 3-D film starring Michael Jackson as **Captain EO** at CinéMagique.

11.45 a.m. Walk back to **Sleeping Beauty's Castle** and cut into Adventureland through the

Bazaar. Don't be tempted to go to **Indiana Jones and the Temple of Peril** yet (unless the queues are minimal), because you're going to do that first thing tomorrow morning. Instead, spend some time exploring **Adventure Isle**, a children's playground of giant proportions. Taking **Captain Hook's Pirate Ship** as your starting point, explore the maze of tunnels, caves, swing-bridges and underground waterfalls. Don't forget your camera.

12.30 p.m. Time for lunch at **Colonel Hathi's Outpost**, a fast-food restaurant serving pizzas and pasta in a jungle setting.

1 p.m. Digest your food by walking round to **Pirates of the Caribbean** at the other end of Adventureland. The 12-minute indoor boat ride through pirate-invaded territory is deceptively calm at the outset – but there are plenty of thrills and comic scenes ahead as you follow the trail of havoc left by the wayward pirates.

1.45 a.m. Book a table for dinner at 7.30 p.m. at the **Blue Lagoon** restaurant which you will have seen as you passed through on the **Pirates of the Caribbean** ride. Return to the fabulously atmospheric **Adventureland Bazaar**, full of colourful clothes and bric-a-brac from exotic countries. Take time to watch the craftsmen at work and admire the exquisite mosaics.

2.30 p.m. Leave Adventureland through the main entrance leading to Central Plaza and head for the stunningly ornate **Sleeping Beauty's Castle**.

See the smoke-breathing dragon in the dungeon and the Disney tapestries and stained-glass windows in the gallery upstairs.

2.55 p.m. Take your place at Central Plaza for the 3 p.m. **Parade** of Disney characters.

3.30 p.m. Stop for coffee and cakes at the **Cable-Car Bake Shop** or enjoy an ice-cream at **Gibson Girl's Ice Cream Parlour**. Then walk off the calories by making for Frontierland, through the imposing fortress gates off Central Plaza. Don't be tempted by **Big Thunder Mountain** – the queues for the trains will be at their longest. Instead, head for **Phantom Manor**, and embark on a chilling journey round the haunted house in a swivelling carriage. This is one of the most imaginative rides at Disneyland Paris. Expect to queue for a while, but most of the waiting area is under cover and there's lots to watch below you.

4.30 p.m. Spend a little while wandering around Frontierland where there is always plenty to watch, such as cowboy shoot-outs, the **Molly Brown Steamboat**, and the screaming crowds on **Thunder Mountain**. You'll have more time to explore tomorrow.

5 p.m. Take your seat at **C'est Magique** at the Fantasy Festival Stage in Fantasyland – Disney characters mime along to Disney's boppiest songs in a first-rate professional revue.

5.30 p.m. Time to explore Fantasyland! As you've got plenty of time, resist the temptation to join the queues for the rides based on the well-loved European tales (**Snow White, Pinocchio** and **Peter Pan**). Instead, savour the atmosphere of the most picturesque of the four lands. If the queues are not off-putting, try a quick ride on the lavishly painted horses of **Le Carousel de Lancelot** (Lancelot's Roundabout) or take to the skies with **Dumbo the Flying Elephant** (both designed with the under-sevens in mind). The queues are never too bad for the **Mad Hatter's Teacups**, a typical fairground ride which whirls you round and round in giant cups. Alternatively, if it's sunny, you can wander round **Alice's Curious Labyrinth**, a complex maze leading to the **Queen of Hearts' Castle**. You may also enjoy the leisurely boat cruise **Le Pays des Contes de Fées** through Storybook Land and its intricate miniatures.

7.30 p.m. Dinner at **Blue Lagoon**.

9 p.m. Time for a quick after-dinner stroll. Disneyland Paris is even more magical in the dark. Particularly spectacular are Adventureland, with its flaming torches and exotic bazaar, and Main Street, USA, with all its intricately designed buildings lit up.

9.20 p.m. Find a good spot on Main Street to watch the **Electrical Parade**. (This is only on at weekends and Bank Holidays).

10 p.m. Wait around to watch the fireworks being let off over **Sleeping Beauty's Castle**. These really are spectacular.

Still got some energy left? Leave the park and head for Festival Disney, where things only start livening up after dusk. If you're in the mood for a cocktail and the chance to boogie down, try **Hurricane's Disco**. If country music is more your scene, there are live bands at **Billy Bob's**, where you can join the crowd at the bar or enjoy a late meal at one of the tables. Don't overdo it, though – remember, you have a full day tomorrow!

Day Two

8.45 a.m. Arrive at the gates.

8.55 a.m. Head up Main Street, USA, to **Casey's Corner**. Turn left and wait at the side entrance to Frontierland.

9.00 a.m. When the barrier is lifted, walk quickly through the tunnel leading to Frontierland, turn left at the **Lucky Nugget Saloon** and then right, towards the entrance to **Big Thunder Mountain**. If you get there promptly, you should board the runaway mining train almost straight away.

9.20 a.m. Walk quickly through Frontierland to the other high-thrill ride in Adventureland – **Indiana Jones and the Temple of Peril**.

10 a.m. Time for another go on **Pirates of the Caribbean** which should still be fairly quiet at this time of day. Then walk back towards the **Bazaar** and climb up the Swiss Family Robinson Tree-House. This 90-foot tree is, from its roots to its leaves, entirely man-made. All the tree-house

rooms are packed with detail and you have a superb view of Adventureland from the top.

11 a.m. Return to the **Bazaar** and walk around **Le Passage Enchanté d'Aladdin** – a series of indoor tableaux depicting scenes from the animated feature film, *Aladdin*.

Time to decide where you want to have dinner tonight. We suggest you either spend the evening Wild West-style at **Buffalo Bill's Show** (6.30 p.m. and 9 p.m.) which is expensive, but offers great entertainment; or else you have a quieter more sophisticated meal at **Auberge de Cendrillon** in Fantasyland or at **Walt's** restaurant in Main Street, USA. Bookings for Buffalo Bill should be made now at City Hall (Main Street, USA), or go direct to the Auberge or Walt's to make your table reservations.

11.30 a.m. Now dinner has been decided, what about lunch? If you want a table-service restaurant, walk into Frontierland and catch Lilly's Follies cancan show at the **Lucky Nugget Saloon** (set menu 80F adults, 40F children) at 11.45 a.m. Alternatively, walk through the **Bazaar** into Fantasyland and take a look at the beautiful **Sleeping Beauty's Castle**. Climb upstairs to see the tapestries and stained-glass windows and then go into the dungeon to meet the dragon. Then go to **Café Hyperion** in Videopolis (Discoveryland) and have a snack lunch (burgers, sandwiches or salads) before taking your seat for the 12.30 performance of **Beauty and the Beast** – a musical show featuring highlighted scenes from the animated feature.

1 p.m. If you've been watching **Beauty and the Beast** spend the next hour doing any of your favourite rides, such as **Space Mountain**, again in Discoveryland. If you're at the **Lucky Nugget**, go back to **Phantom Manor** – it's still as spooky the second time!

2 p.m. If it's dry (and, even better, if it's sunny), ease back into the action after lunch by going on the **Indian Canoes** in Frontierland. (You may like to catch the **Disneyland Paris Railroad** train from Discoveryland to Frontierland if you've just been on **Space Mountain**). The canoes are a more energetic way of navigating the waterways around **Big Thunder Mountain** than the paddle-wheelers or keelboats – and you'll see more.

2.45 p.m. Take time to explore the parts of Frontierland that you haven't already seen. Try your shooting skill at the **Shootin' Gallery** for 10F a round. The **Cottonwood Creek Ranch** will give you the atmosphere of a small farmhold-ing, with real animals instead of the animatronic variety.

2.50 p.m. If you missed out on the **Parade** yester-day, take your place on Central Plaza for a grand-stand view. Alternatively, this is the time to grab a seat aboard the kiddies' favourites in Fantasyland, while junior is propped up on Dad's shoulders watching the **Parade**.

3.30 p.m. It's a Small World! (Fantasyland) is the best known of all the Disney rides, and worth try-ing once even if you do find it a little twee.

4 p.m. Afternoon tea? Treat yourself to some Victorian elegance behind the velvet swagged curtains in **Plaza Gardens**, or at a pavement table outside if it's sunny.

4.45 p.m. If you've reserved a seat for **Buffalo Bill's** 6.30 p.m. show, your day in the park is drawing to a close. You've got time to do some last-minute shopping or perhaps queue for one of your favourite rides, before heading out through the gates for the last time. (If you've booked for the later performance, why not head back to your hotel for a shower? Don't be tempted to eat, however – there will be plenty on your plate during the show!)

5.30 p.m. If you're going to **Buffalo Bill's** (you should arrive there by 6.15 p.m. as the show starts promptly at 6.30 p.m.), you can spend 45 minutes walking around Festival Disney where there are lots of shops and bars. Alternatively, if you are eating in the park, you may like an hour or so in Festival Disney before you return for your dinner and more rides.

Hope you enjoyed yourself!

THE WHIRLWIND TOUR FOR FAMILIES WITH YOUNG CHILDREN

This one-day tour has been specially designed to cater for families with young children. The rides are particularly suitable for 4–7 year olds, although older children will also enjoy them. The tour centres mainly round Fantasyland as this is the best place for children of this age. See Chapter Ten: Taking Young Children to Disneyland Paris, for further tips and advice on touring with children. It's unrealistic to devise a set itinerary for children under four years old, so, if your children fall into this age category, see our suggested Top Rides and Attractions for Toddlers on page 195.

8.45 a.m. Arrive at the gates and buy your tickets. Children under 12 pay a reduced rate.

8.55 a.m. Walk up Main Street, USA, to queue at the entrance to Fantasyland (just to the right of **Sleeping Beauty's Castle**).

9 a.m. Walk quickly through Fantasyland to **Peter Pan's Flight**, avoiding the temptation to stop and look at any of the pretty buildings. **Peter Pan's Flight** is the most popular children's ride in Disneyland Paris, so you want to do it early before the queues build up.

9.20 a.m. Cross over to **Dumbo the Flying Elephant** for an outdoor flying trip.

9.30 a.m. Enter the world of **Snow White and the Seven Dwarfs** in a short, indoor journey through the witch's territory. If you are with very young or nervous children, it is better to take them to **Pinocchio's Adventures** next door – a similar, but less frightening ride.

9.40 a.m. Walk over to **It's A Small World!**, on the other side of Fantasyland. This is a wonderful ride for small children – an indoor boat journey through the countries of the world, represented by dancing, singing dolls in national costume. Before you exit, spend a few minutes looking round the village of model houses. The windows are all at different heights for the children to peer through.

10.15 a.m. Time for a rest and drink at the **Old Mill**, stopping off at the toilets next to **Pizzeria Bella Notte** (opposite **It's A Small World!**) if required!

10.45 a.m. Brighten up your morning with a whirl on the **Mad Hatter's Teacups**, a classic fairground ride that spins you round and round in giant cups.

11.15 a.m. Walk round **Alice's Curious Labyrinth** to the **Queen of Hearts' Castle**. Listen out for the squeaks and whistles from the hedges and look for the Alice characters peering at you from corners. Parents will want to have their cameras ready as there are some excellent vantage points from the castle.

11.45 a.m. Time for one more ride before lunch. Either jump aboard **Casey Junior** – a train ride through Storybook Land with some very gentle roller-coaster effects, or cruise through the same Storybook Land on a boat. All the family will enjoy the beautiful miniature scenes derived from international folklore and Disney films.

12.15 p.m. Lunch at **Toad Hall** restaurant, an old English baronial-style home specialising in fish and chips, or at **Au Châlet de la Marionette** for a burger or roast chicken and chips.

1.15 p.m. Visit **Sleeping Beauty's Castle**, the central landmark of Fantasyland. Climb upstairs to see the tapestries and beautiful stained-glass windows. Don't forget to go downstairs, too, and see the dragon (very young children may be scared).

1.45 p.m. Have a look at some of the Fantasyland shops. If you want to buy your child a fancy-dress costume, **La Chaumière des Sept Nains** is the place to go. Alternatively, go to **La Confiserie des Trois Fées**, a pretty sweet shop – look out for the fairies floating in the chimney.

2.30 p.m. Now's the time to decide about this evening's plans. The park is even more magical at night, so it is worth keeping the children up for a special treat. If you want entertainment with dinner, book a table at the **Lucky Nugget Saloon** in Frontierland. Alternatively, **Walt's** in Main Street is ideally positioned for the evening **Electrical Parade**. Or you can save money by buying a fast-food snack at **Café Hyperion** in Videopolis, Discoveryland, and then watching the brilliant **Beauty and the Beast Show**.

2.45 p.m. Find a good spot for the Disney **Parade**. This will be one of the highlights of your child's day so it is worth getting there early for a kerbside seat at the Central Plaza end of Main Street.

3 p.m. Disney **Parade**.

3.30 p.m. Time for tea and cakes at the **Cable-Car Bake Shop** or an ice-cream at the **Gibson Girl's**

Ice-Cream Parlour in Main Street, USA.

4 p.m. Walk down Main Street, away from **Sleeping Beauty's Castle**, looking at any shops that catch your interest.

4.30 p.m. All aboard the **Disneyland Paris Railroad** which takes about 25 minutes to chug around the park – a good opportunity to rest tired, little feet. Get off at the first stop (**Frontierland Depôt**) or, if your children are enjoying the ride and rest, continue on the train and get off at this stop the next time round.

5.15 p.m. Visit **Cottonwood Creek Ranch** (it closes at dusk). Small children will enjoy the opportunity to stroke the livestock who roam freely in this little farm.

5.45 p.m. Walk leisurely round Frontierland, watching the screaming crowds on **Thunder Mountain** and the boats and the canoes on the water.

6 p.m. Continue round to **Phantom Manor**, the spooky house at the top of the hill (very young children may find this too scarey).

7 p.m. Dinner at your chosen restaurant. (Note that show times may vary, so you may need to alter your eating time accordingly.)

8.30 p.m. Time for some last-minute magic by jumping astride one of the beautifully ornate horses on **Le Carousel de Lancelot** in

Fantasyland. You may like to re-ride the other rides in Fantasyland which your children particularly enjoyed. Make sure you take your place in Main Street at 9.15 p.m. for the 9.30 p.m. **Electrical Parade**.

10 p.m. **Fantasia in the Sky**. Look up above **Sleeping Beauty's Castle** to see the most wonderful fireworks display.

THE TWO-DAY TOUR FOR FAMILIES WITH YOUNG CHILDREN

This more leisurely two-day tour has been specially designed to cater for families with young children. The rides are particularly suitable for 4–7 year olds, although older children will also enjoy them. If you have younger children in tow, see our suggested Top Rides and Attractions for Toddlers on page 195.

Day One

8.45 a.m. Arrive at the gates and buy two-day passports for all the family (reduced rates for under-12s).

8.55 a.m. Walk up Main Street, USA, to queue at the Fantasyland entrance to the right of **Sleeping Beauty's Castle**.

9 a.m. Walk straight round to **Peter Pan's Flight** – a wonderful journey over the rooftops of London to Never-Never-Land. Later in the day, the queues are horrendous for this ride.

9.20 a.m. Take to the skies with **Dumbo the Flying Elephant**.

9.30 a.m. Go to **Snow White and the Seven Dwarfs** or **Pinocchio's Adventures** if you are with younger, more nervous children. The Snow White ride is actually quite scarey, focusing on the wicked witch scenes.

9.45 a.m. Walk into Adventureland. Most people will still be lingering in Main Street, USA, so now is the time to do the wonderful **Pirates of the Caribbean** indoor boat ride.

10.15 a.m. Visit **Le Coffre du Capitaine**, a shop next door to **Pirates of the Caribbean**, that specialises in pirate wear and gimmicks for the children.

10.30 a.m. Walk over the precarious plank bridges to **Adventure Isle**. This island is great fun for children to explore, with lots of tunnels, underground caves and a shuddering suspension bridge overlooking the wrecked galleon. For some good photographs, walk up to **Spyglass Hill** which has several good vantage points over Adventureland.

11 a.m. Stop for a rest and refreshments at **Captain Hook's Galley**.

11.30 a.m. Walk over to the southside of the island and climb the Swiss Family Robinson Tree-House, a 90ft tree, totally man-made from its roots to its leaves.

noon. Now's the time to book dinner for tonight (7 p.m.). Your children may have spotted the **Blue Lagoon** restaurant which you pass through on the **Pirates of the Caribbean** ride, or the pretty **Auberge du Cendrillon** (Fantasyland) which has Cinderella's carriage standing outside. If you are on a budget, there are also plenty of cheaper fast-food restaurants to eat in (see page 141 for restaurant reviews).

12.15 p.m. Walk through to Frontierland and have lunch at the **Cowboy Cookout Barbeque**. This is great fun for children as there's lot of space to run around, and there's a live country band to dance to.

1.15 p.m. Digest your food by strolling over to **Cottonwood Creek Ranch** where young children will enjoy stroking the livestock who are allowed to roam free in this spotless little farm.

1.45 p.m. Time for some action! If it's a sunny day, the **Indian Birchbark Canoes** provide a fun way to explore the **Rivers of the Wild West**. If the weather is not so good, you may prefer the shelter of the **Mark Twain** or **Molly Brown Steamboats**.

2.15 p.m. Stroll leisurely through Frontierland towards Central Plaza, taking in the Wild West atmosphere and watching all the goings on, such as **Big Thunder Mountain Railroad** and the cowboy shoot-outs on top of the **Lucky Nugget Saloon**.

2.45 p.m. Find a good kerbside spot at Central Plaza for the Disney **Parade**.

3 p.m. Disney **Parade** – this will be one of the main highlights of your child's day.

3.30 p.m. Stop for tea at the **Cable-Car Bake Shop** or enjoy an ice-cream at the **Gibson Girl's Ice-Cream Parlour**.

4 p.m. Spend some time looking at the shops in Main Street, USA. You may like to have a family portrait photo taken at Main Street Motors, depicting you all in Victorian costumes behind the wheel of a vintage car.

4.30 p.m. Take a ride back up Main Street, USA, to Central Plaza aboard one of the old-fashioned **Main Street Vehicles**, such as the horse-drawn streetcar, which depart from Town Square. Walk into Fantasyland again.

5 p.m. Take your seat for **C'est Magique** at the Fantasy Festival Stage. You and your children will love this lively first-rate professional revue in which Disney characters mime along to Disney's boppiest tunes.

5.30 p.m. Go for a late afternoon whirl on the **Mad Hatter's Teacups**.

5.45 p.m. You now have just over an hour to look at the shops, re-ride some of your children's favourites or just walk around and take in the magical atmosphere.

7 p.m. Dinner at the restaurant of your choice.

8.30 p.m. Adventureland, with its flaming torches and ornate **Bazaar**, is particularly exotic at night, so it is a good place for a walk. If your children are still crying out for action, take them for a quick ride on **Le Carousel de Lancelot** in Fantasyland.

9.15 p.m. Find a good kerbside spot for this evening's **Electrical Parade** which starts at Central Plaza.

9.30 p.m. **Electrical Parade**.

10 p.m. Don't forget to look up at the skies for the wonderful **Fantasia** firework display.

Day Two

8.50 a.m. As you have a two-day passport, you should be able to walk straight into the park.

8.55 a.m. Start the day with a train ride around the park aboard the **Disneyland Paris Railroad**. Beat the queues by getting to the station platform early.

9.20 a.m. Arrive back at Main Street, USA. Walk leisurely down Main Street, USA, stopping to take photos and to windowshop.

9.45 a.m. Walk across Fantasyland to **It's A Small World!**, a wonderful indoor boat ride, through the countries of the world, represented by pretty, dancing, singing dolls in national costume. Stop to look around the model village on your way out.

10.15 a.m. Now try the **Pirouettes du Vieux Moulin**, a very gentle Ferris wheel that gives you fantastic views over Fantasyland.

10.30 a.m. Walk round to **Alice's Curious Labyrinth**. Tell your children to listen for squeaks and squeals and to look out for characters peering at them from behind the hedges. At the centre of the labyrinth is the **Queen of Hearts' Castle**, which has some excellent vantage points for taking photos.

10.45 a.m. Time for a drink at **March Hare Refreshments** or try a yoghurt drink at the Old Mill.

11 a.m. Time to explore Storybook Land. Either jump aboard **Casey Junior** – a train ride with some very gentle roller-coaster effects – or cruise through the same Storybook Land on a boat. All the family will enjoy the beautiful miniature scenes depicted from international folklore and Disney films. You may find the kids want to try both!

11.30 a.m. Walk over to **Sleeping Beauty's Castle**. Look at the tapestries and stained-glass windows upstairs and, if your children are old and brave enough, take them down to the cellar where a dragon lurks.

noon. Time to decide about this evening's plans. If you want a fun night out, **Buffalo Bill's Wild West Show** (Festival Disney) is superb. There are two shows – 6.30 p.m. and 9 p.m. You can make your reservation at City Hall (Main Street) or in person at the Buffalo Bill booking office in Festival Disney. Children will love this show which stars 40 cowboys and Indians and over 80 horses, buffalo and longhorn steer. If you want a cheaper night's entertainment in the park, book at the **Lucky Nugget Saloon**, a Wild West-pantomime dinner show with cancan dancers. Whichever you choose, make your reservation now. Alternatively, you could save money by eating at any of the fast-food restaurants in the park (see page 141 for reviews).

12.15 p.m. Walk into the futuristic Discoveryland and take your seat for the superb **Beauty and the Beast Show** in Videopolis. If you want a seat near the front, you'll have to eat afterwards at one of the tables higher up. The show starts at 12.30 p.m.

1.15 p.m. Take to the skies in **Orbitron**, Discoveryland's version of **Dumbo the Flying Elephant!**

1.30 p.m. Look round the **Star Traders** shop which sells all sorts of *Star Wars* gifts and toys.

1.45 p.m. Older children may be unable to resist trying **Star Tours**, a six-minute simulated journey into space. There is a height restriction for this and it is not really suitable for the under-sevens, so one parent may want to wait in one of the cafés. Similarly, the 3-D film **Captain EO** is great fun for bigger children, but the villainess may prove too much for younger ones!

2.30 p.m. Walk back across the park to Frontierland, stopping off to take photos, look at shops or re-do any rides on your way.

3.15 p.m. Go to **Phantom Manor**, the spooky house on the top of the hill (very young children may find this too frightening and be happier to watch the Disney **Parade** again).

3.45 p.m. Take a trip round the **Rivers of the Far West** aboard the **River Rogue Keelboats**. Again, families may wish to split at this point with the older children and one parent going off to try **Big Thunder Railroad**. There is a height restriction for this ride and the queues may be very big. If it looks too long a wait, come back and do this after dinner.

4.15 p.m. You will now have seen the best attractions in the park for families. Use the next hour or two before dinner to shop, re-do rides or catch up on any that you have missed. Hope you had fun!

5.30 p.m. Exit from the park (remember to have your hand stamped if you're planning to return), and walk around Festival Disney with its shops, bars and arcade machines. Arrive by 6.15 p.m. for **Buffalo Bill's Wild West Show**, or return at leisure to the park for your evening meal.

THE PHOTOGRAPHER'S TOUR

You are not allowed to take flash shots on the interior rides. Cameras and video cameras can be hired at Town Square Photography in Main

Street, USA, but resist the temptation of leaving undeveloped film there as the processing prices are ridiculously high.

Some of the more obvious vantage points in the park are marked with Kodak Photo Spot signs. Following is our personal selection of the top places to get a good shot. Although the guide is aimed at the stills photographer, the vantage points suggested are obviously just as useful for the video enthusiast.

1. Main Street, USA

For a general view, looking towards Sleeping Beauty's Castle, perch on the bandstand in Town Square. Watch for the Disney characters while in this area – Mickey, Minnie and Donald can be found greeting the arrivals filing through the turnstiles. Don't be afraid to shout and wave to attract their attention – they've made a career out of posing for the camera, after all! The façades in Main Street are all worth photographing; in particular, the Market House Delicatessen and the Gibson Girl's Ice-Cream Parlour. Try to get one of the passing veteran cars into the frame for added atmosphere. If you're photographing people, there are usually some parked vehicles ideal for posing beside – or inside!

2. Sleeping Beauty's Castle

Avoid standing in front of the main entrance for your portrait shot – you'll end up with a frame full of people's backs! Instead, step round to the left-hand side of the castle (next to Adventureland), where you'll have a wonderful view of the castle rising above the grassy embankment, with the reflected image in the moat below. Be careful not to chop off the highest turret! Inside the Castle, walk up to the gallery and use your flash to capture the ornate ceiling. The pretty stained-glass windows are worth taking close-up, especially Sleeping Beauty receiving her princely kiss.

4. Frontierland

The best vantage point from which to photograph all the action in Frontierland (and there's a lot to capture in one frame) is from the Crypt behind Phantom Manor. Because it's at the top of a flight of steps, you can look down on the water below. If you're patient, you'll soon have a keelboat, paddle-ship or a canoe sail into the frame, with Big Thunder Mountain in the background. A silhouette of Phantom Manor against a cloudy sky from this point can look rather menacing, while the shoot-out outside the Lucky Nugget Saloon will provide you with lots of action shots. (Don't miss the bandits on the roof!) For picturesque scenes of turn-of-the-century life back at the ranch, take some shots by the duck pond outside the Cottonwood Creek Ranch, with the windmill in the background.

4. Adventureland

The Moroccan-style entrance to Adventureland is the most photogenic of the four avenues which lead from Central Plaza, especially on a sunny day. With the palm trees and sandy embankments, you could easily be in North Africa! Inside, there are plenty of vantage points in the Bazaar to take atmospheric pictures, although most opt for the area immediately beyond the entrance, by the deserted Land-Rover.

The next location stop is Adventure Isle. Climb up to the middle of the suspension bridge for great views of the wrecked galleon and of Captain Hook's Pirate Ship. There is also lots of atmosphere amidst the branches and leaves of the Swiss Family Robinson Tree-House, and don't miss the faces of the people setting of on the Indiana Jones and the Temple of Peril ride with its 360-degree loop.

5. Fantasyland

If you have children, this is the place you'll want to capture their gleeful faces as they try out the rides. The Mad Hatter's Teacups is an ideal setting – it's colourful and there's lots of room to manoeuvre inside the cups built for four. Dumbo is best photographed from outside the railings while the youngsters whizz past you. Alternatively, take your camera with you on the ride for an elephant's eye view of one of the prettiest corners of Disneyland Paris. Another good ride to take photos from is on the Pirouettes du Vieux Moulin. Elsewhere, the façade to Sir Mickey's shop, with its giant curly beanstalk, makes a fun picture; Toad Hall is an elegant pastiche of an English baronial hall; and the Queen of Hearts' Castle inside the Labyrinth offers another vantage point from up high.

6. Discoveryland

Don't miss the amazing new Space Mountain construction with the cannon that emits smoke and a loud bang every time a space ship is catapulted up into the galaxy. The airship suspended above Videopolis is also an impressive sight to capture, particularly if you can frame it against a blue sky. For a more futuristic image, there's the *Star Wars* craft, posed as if in mid-battle outside the entrance to Star Tours. Finally, Orbitron is the obvious landmark which begs to be photographed, from the ground or from one of the circling spheres.

CHAPTER THIRTEEN

EXCURSIONS

Although Disneyland Paris is a world in itself, it is always fun to explore the surrounding countryside. The following are a selection of day excursions, plus a guide to the capital city of Paris, which is only about 35 minutes away by the RER network.

How to get to Disneyland Paris

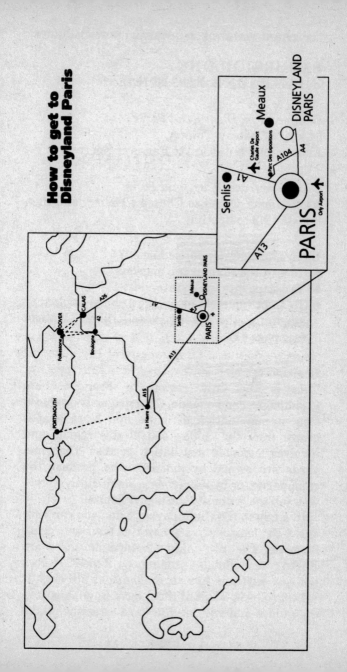

EXCURSION ONE
CHAMPAGNE REGION

Distance from Disneyland Paris:
54 km to Château-Thierry.
Approximately 100 km to Reims or Epernay.

Directions from Disneyland Paris:
A4 to Reims. Or A4 to Château-Thierry and then
take the N3 to Epernay

Why go to the Champagne Region?
● To visit the champagne maisons.
● To escape into the countryside.
● To treat yourself to a night or two of luxury
  staying at the superb Hostellerie du Château
  (see page 61).

Description
This is the only region in France where
Champagne can be made. Champagne is produced
from a combination of white and black grapes
grown from the chalky soil of this region, and
involves a double distillation process. The vine-
yards are owned by *maisons* who produce the
champagne, or by *vignerons* – small cultivators –
who sell the grapes to the bigger houses.

In a trip to the Champagne region you can visit
one of the *maisons* to see how this luxurious drink
is made. The two main Champagne cities are
Epernay and Reims (pronounced Rance). It does
not cost anything to visit the *maisons* although it
is best to book. Most of them have English-speaking guides and will let you have a tasting. Make

sure you wear warm clothing as it does get chilly down in the depths of the vaults.

One of the most famous Champagne *maisons* is Moët et Chandon in Epernay, which has 28 km of subterranean vaults. Nearby is the Mercier *maison*. There is also a Champagne museum in Epernay.

There are several Champagne houses in Reims (the City of Coronations), as well as the beautiful thirteenth-century Nôtre Dame cathedral, where 37 kings of France were crowned.

Further Information
Moët et Chandon, 20 Avenue de Champagne, Epernay (Tel: 26 54 71 11)
Mercier, 70 Avenue de Champagne, Epernay (Tel: 26 54 75 26)
Pommery, 5 Place General Gouraud, Reims (Tel: 26 61 62 55)
Veuve Clicquot, 1 Place des Droits-des-Hommes, Reims (Tel: 26 40 25 42)
Mumm, 34 Rue du Champ-de-Mars, Reims (Tel: 26 49 59 70)

Tourist Offices
Reims: 2 Rue Guillaume-de-Machault (Tel: 26 47 25 69)
Epernay: 7 Ave de Champagne (Tel: 26 55 33 00)

EXCURSION TWO
CHANTILLY

Distance from Disneyland Paris:
About 50 km.

Directions from Disneyland Paris:
A4 east from Paris, exit Meaux, then take the
N330 to Senlis and the D924 on to Chantilly.

Why go to Chantilly?
● To visit Chantilly Château.
● To see the horse-racing.
● To visit the horse and pony museum.
● For shopping.
● For walks in the forest.

Description
After visiting Sleeping Beauty's Castle (Le
Château de la Belle au Bois Dormant), why not
drive out to the French countryside and see a real
French château in Chantilly? This magical castle
is reached across a moat guarded by two beautiful,
bronze hunting hounds.

The Chantilly estate dates back to the tenth
century and was bought in the late fourteenth century by the Chancellor of France, Pierre
d'Orgemont, who, together with his son, Amaury,
rebuilt the castle into a fortress with seven
towers. Amaury never had children, so when he
died the estate passed to his sister Marguerite,
wife of Philippe de Montmorency. It was the
Montmorency family and the Condés (also related
to the Orgemonts through marriage) who had the
most influence on the Chantilly estate.

Constable Anne de Montmorency was a very
wealthy man (at one time he owned over a hun-
dred castles and estates) and he commissioned
Pierre Champiges to renovate the château in the
French Renaissance style. The Constable also had
the Petit Château (little castle) built which was

originally separated from the main château by water.

Unfortunately, the main castle was destroyed during the Revolution, and was not restored until the late nineteenth century when it was owned by the Duke of Aumale (the fourth son of King Louis-Philippe). The Duke insisted that the architecture of the château should not be modified in any way. On his death, he left his art collections and the estate to the Institut de France and the castle is now a museum housing these collections. The Petit Château still stands and now houses the Duke of Aumale's library. However, only two of the seven chapels which were built by Constable Anne de Montmorency are still standing today.

The Condé museum was created by the Duke of Aumale and now houses hundreds of paintings and several thousand drawings. These include some Raphaels and a Fillipino Lippi, and there are also miniatures from a fifteenth-century *Book of Hours* which has been attributed to Jean Fouquet.

The highlight of the museum is *Les Très Riches Heures du Duc du Berry*, the most famous of all *Book of Hours*, which is housed in the library, the Cabinet des Livres. You can only see this with a guide.

There are plenty of other things to see and do in Chantilly. Only five minutes walk away is the Musée Vivant du Cheval (Living Horse Museum), housed in the giant stables. This was built in 1719 by Louis-Henri de Bourbon, the seventh Prince of Condé, who believed that he would be reincarnated as a horse and so was obviously keen to provide good accommodation for his future relatives! The stables housed 240 horses and up to 500 hounds. The Musée Vivant du Cheval was founded in 1982 by a riding master called Yves Bienaime. This private museum comprises a series of rooms, each with its own educational and horse-related theme. For example, one room portrays the blacksmith's trade, and another is a veterinary's operating-room. Various tack-rooms and displays of children's toy horses complete the ensemble.

If you are not a horse buff, these exhibits will be rather dull and you will probably prefer wandering around the stalls and looking at the beautiful horses – which you will later see performing in a dressage-based demonstration in the central arena. In this equine display, talented riders show off the skills of Andalusian and Portuguese horses, similar to those ridden by the princes in the eighteenth century when the stables were built. During the Christmas holidays, there is a particularly lavish show which is great fun for children.

If you are interested in a bit of a flutter, there is also a racecourse in Chantilly. Alternatively, take a walk around the town itself which is full of chic boutiques and restaurants. Le Restaurant du Château in Rue du Connetable is a lively, atmospheric place to stop for a three-course lunch, which you can then walk off in the nearby woods of Chantilly.

Further Information
Office de Tourisme, 23 Avenue du Marechal, Chantilly (Tel: 44 57 08 58)

EXCURSION THREE
FONTAINEBLEAU

Distance from Disneyland Paris:
63 km.

Directions from Disneyland Paris:
A4 towards Paris, then exit Emerainville/Melun (N104). Drive to Melun, then take N6 to Fontainebleau.

Why go to Fontainebleau?
- To visit the château of Fontainebleau.
- To visit the arty village of Barbizon.
- For walking, cycling, climbing or horseriding in the forest.
- For peace and quiet.
- To see Vaux-le-Vicomte (see Excursion Seven).

Description
After an action-packed stay at Disneyland Paris, Fontainebleau is the ideal place to relax and unwind either for a day trip or extended part of your holiday.

The town of Fontainebleau is very attractive and full of restaurants, Parisian-style cafés and chic boutiques. Or, if you prefer to stay a little more off the beaten track, try the nearby village of Samois-sur-Seine, where there is a very good, reasonably priced hotel called Hostellerie du Country Club (see page 60) on the river.

Fontainebleau is dominated by the huge, sprawling château with Disney-like façades. Originally a hunting lodge, this dates back to the twelfth century, and many of the great kings seem to have made their mark on it over the years. It was particularly influenced by François I, who used Italian renaissance craftsmen to work on the interiors of the château in the sixteenth century. The Gallery of François I, by Italian artist Rosso, is a fine example of renaissance art. Napoleon Bonaparte also had a big influence on the château and actually signed his abdication there on 6 April 1814. Two weeks later, on 20 April, Napoleon bade farewell to his troops at the top of the sweeping horseshoe staircase. The château now houses the Napoleon I Museum which occupies a series of rooms on the ground level and on the first floor of the Louis XV wing.

The beautiful gardens of the château can also be visited. The Garden of Diana is named after the famous fountain statue of Diana hunting, although the original is now in the Louvre (the one in the garden is a bronze copy).

About five kilometres from Fontainebleau is the pretty but touristy village of Barbizon where landscape artists, such as Jean-Francois Millet and Theodore Rousseau, and writers, such as George Sand, found inspiration. There is one long, main high street, full of villas, restaurants and hotels – all proudly bearing commemorative plaques of the artists who lived there. The Ancienne Auberge du Père Ganne (Father Ganne's Old Inn) used to be a grocery, run by Father Ganne, which offered cheap lodgings for artists. It is now a museum showing how they lived and exhibiting some of their landscape paintings. Further along the high street is the old barn which Rousseau used as a studio, and which is now converted into the Barbizon School Municipal Museum, housing work by Barbizon masters such as Rousseau, Dupré and Jacue and their disciples (Ortmans, Ciceri, Gassies, Chaigneau and de Penne). It will not take you long to tour this tiny museum. Afterwards, you can stroll round the village looking at works by contemporary artists and craftsmen, before stopping for lunch in one of the many traditional village restaurants.

The Fontainebleau forest, once a royal hunting ground, is now frequented by rosy-cheeked walkers, cyclists, riders and climbers. The local riding school is at 29 Rue de l'Arbre Sec and provides tuition and trekking in the forest.

Further Information
Tourist Office, 31 Place Napoléon Bonaparte (Tel: 64 22 25 68)

EXCURSION FOUR
PARC ASTERIX

Distance from Disneyland Paris:
40 km.

Directions from Disneyland Paris:
A4 to Meaux, N330 to Ermenonville, then DN22 to the A1 (northbound, Lille direction). Parc Asterix is signposted just a few kilometres up the A1.

Stopping off en route
If you are going to Parc Asterix with children, you won't have much time to spare, as it will take most of the day to explore the theme park. If you do want to combine half a day at Parc Asterix with a

few hours sightseeing, stop off to see the cathedral at Meaux which dates back to the twelfth century or visit the pretty village of Ermenonville to see the eighteenth-century château, the park where Rousseau died and the island in the lake where he was later buried. (Rousseau's body is no longer there as he was moved to the Pantheon during the Revolution.)

Why go to Parc Asterix?
- To see the French alternative to Disneyland Paris.
- To experience French culture and history in theme-park format.
- For roller-coaster and fairground-style rides.
- For a fun day for little children exploring Asterix village.

Description
If Disneyland Paris has whetted your appetite for theme parks, Parc Asterix is only 30 minutes drive away, and well worth a visit, as it is so different from its American counterpart. The whole park, set in the heart of a 155-hectare forest, is based around the adventures of the French comic strip, Asterix, which was created by two Frenchmen, René Goscinny and Albert Uderzo, in the late 1950s.

The theme park opened in April 1989 and, until Disneyland Paris, was the biggest in France, attracting over one million visitors each year. Smaller than Disneyland Paris, Parc Asterix does not have on-site hotels, so most visitors are day-trippers from Paris or other parts of France – although there are always staff on hand who speak English.

The opening of Disneyland Paris obviously throws a cloud over the future of this French theme park. 'We were worried about Disney for the first year,' a Parc Asterix representative admitted, 'but then, we are very different from Disney.'

They certainly are like chalk and cheese. Parc Asterix is as French as Disney is American. If you are expecting the sophistication, slickness and high-tech animatronics of Disney, you will feel short-changed at Parc Asterix. The French park is cruder, yet it is still charming, relying more on the humour of its street performers and side shows, and its offbeat education in the history of France with more of a fairground atmosphere than the American version. You don't find anything as stomach-churning at Disneyland Paris as the giant roller-coaster at Parc Asterix. You also don't find anything as fun as the Asterix village for little children to explore.

For those who are not familiar with Goscinny's and Uderzo's comic strip, Asterix is a brave little Gaul, who always wins his battles, even in times of great adversity. The first thing you see when you pull up in the carpark is the funny-looking little character perched on the top of a mountain. Asterix's main ally is roly-poly Obelix with his long red plaits.

Although René Goscinny died in the 1970s, Albert Uderzo has continued producing Asterix books on his own. The stories of Asterix are full of Latin names, jokes and puns – yet both Goscinny and Uderzo claimed they didn't know any Latin at all and had to look it all up! Asterix is written in French but all the titles have been translated into English by Anthea and Derek Hockridge, so if you are planning a trip to the theme park, you or your children may enjoy reading a book or two first to prepare you for the atmosphere and spirit of the Asterix world.

Like Disneyland Paris, Parc Asterix is arranged into different thematic sections, the highlights of which are depicted below. If you want to see and experience all the sections at leisure, you really need a whole day.

Beer and wine are sold in Parc Asterix (alcohol is banned at Disneyland Paris).

VIA ANTIQUA

This is the first section you walk through after entering the gates. Asterix and Obelix are often waiting here to greet you and are happy to offer a hug and to pose for photos! Piped mediaeval music sets the atmosphere as you wander down the main street, lined with shops and snack bars. You'll immediately sample the Asterix humour – the 'Servix' station with its unleaded hay-pumps and the photo shop, 'Touthandeclick'.

All the practical services are found in this area, including an information centre, a place where pushchairs can be hired and coats and luggage checked in, the Credit Latin where you can change currency, a First-Aid Centre, and an office to go to if you have lost your children.

THE ROMAN CITY

Once you get to the top of Via Antiqua you enter the Roman City. Straight ahead of you is the Gladiators' Arena, which immediately transports you into the ancient world of gladiators and barbarians. Twice a day, the Olympic Games are held in this uncovered arena, and it is an attraction not to be missed. Watch where you sit during this 30-minute show! I had the shock of my life when 'something' jumped out from under my seat (you'll see what I mean!).

To the left of the amphitheatre is the Grand Carousel, a Roman version of the traditional merry-go-round. This is fun for little children and adults like myself who still enjoy the magical sensation of gliding round on a brightly painted horse.

You cannot go to ancient Rome without seeing a chariot race and this is depicted in fairground style with Ben Hur's Chariots, alias good old-fashioned bumper cars. Opposite this is one of the most popular attractions – the Descent of the Styx. Expect to queue for this ride, particularly in the heat of the summer, when the thought of plummeting down the rapids in family-size giant rubber rings is most appealing. This is a tame but enjoyable ride, suitable for all ages.

Young children will enjoy the Petitbonum Camp, next to Ben Hur's Chariots. This is an adventure playground, made of wood logs for little Gauls to climb and slide around in.

If you are in need of lunch or a refreshing ice-cream, Caius Cepaderefus is a clean pizza restaurant in the Roman City area, where the service is brisk. Alternatively, you can grab a snack at the fast-food restaurant, Fastes de Rome.

THE ASTERIX VILLAGE
If you have young children, this section is a must – they find it great fun to run in and out of the sixteen huts which were designed by Albert Uderzo and built of stone, wood and thatch. All sorts of

different scenes are depicted in these little dwellings. For example, in one you will find Asterix and Obelix having breakfast together, in another Falbala and Bonnemine are shopping. You can also watch a puppet show, or lean over and listen to the Magic Well.

You can continue your journey through the village by boat. This trip is called the Asterix Run, and although much less sophisticated than Disney's Pirates of the Caribbean, depicts a similar scene of combat in which the Gauls eventually triumph.

Before you leave this section, little children will enjoy the Carute forest with its mini-village, mini-roller-coaster and little train. Listen out for the bird songs (recorded!) in the forest.

THE GREAT LAKE

This depicts the charm of the Mediterranean and houses the largest (2,000 seats) dolphinarium in Europe. Regardless of my own reservations about keeping these beautiful animals in captivity, the show is rather slow-moving for young children, although there are some entertaining highlights – such as the man swimming with the dolphins and when children, taken from the audience, cross the water in a boat towed by the dolphins. Two glossy-black sealions also star in the show. This is always a popular attraction, so be prepared to queue.

For teenagers and thrillseekers, the most exciting ride at Parc Asterix is the Goudurix, at the far side of the lake. This is the largest roller-coaster in Europe and will loop you upside down no less than seven times, travelling at speeds of up to 75 km per hour. Not for the faint hearted!

Another ride for those wanting to experience the sensation of the lake rushing towards them, is the Roman Galley. This is like a giant see-saw over the lake which swings you through 90 degrees.

Afterwards, if your stomach can handle a sit-down meal, the Arcimboldo is a bright, cheerful-looking restaurant, overlooking the lake. This has been designed out of giant, colourful plastic fruit and specialises in grilled food. They also have a junior menu for the under-twelves. If it is a hot day and you just want a sandwich, soft drink or ice-cream, there are snack places by the lake.

THE RUE DE PARIS

From an educational point of view, this is the most interesting section in that you experience different centuries of French history. You enter Paris over the drawbridge by the Great Lake. This leads you to the Mediaeval Square, where some fantastic acrobats, jugglers and tumblers perform. There is also a show called the Court of Miracles inspired by Victor Hugo's *The Hunchback of Nôtre Dame* and starring Esmeralda and Quasimodo. All the shows and films are in French so if you don't speak the language well, you miss out on a lot of the fun. Non-speakers should stick to the more visual shows, such as the acrobats and jugglers.

As you enter inside this section, you come across all the shops depicting crafts of the nineteenth century. This is educational for children who can watch craftsmen demonstrate how the potter, basket-weaver, printer, cabinet-maker, weaver and sculptor used to work. This century is depicted with great vigour and vitality. You can stop to watch the Dances from the Belle Epoque or see the

Artists' Hotel which lights up to show the great men of the century such as Hugo, Moet, Offenbach, Toulouse-Lautrec and Gounod. If you want a souvenir of your visit, you can have your photo taken in period costume at Nicéphore Beloizeau or, instead, visit Le Bonheur des Dames, a recreation of the first department store in Paris.

Young children will love the Animal Studio where they can be made-up as a superstar dog or cat. There is also a film about dogs and cats, all in French, but still fun for children who have pets at home. Alternatively, you can watch a 3-D film on nature in the Great Canadian North – although it falls far short of Captain EO at Disneyland Paris.

If you want to eat in this part of the park, you can dine under the big top at the Restaurant du Cirque.

GERGOVIE SQUARE

If you want to end your day on an upbeat note, you can try the mini-roller-coaster, the Trans-Arverne – tame enough not to terrify Granny. Finally, if it's a hot day and you don't mind leaving the park a little wet, have a final ride on the Big Splash.

Attractions for little Gauls

- The Big Merry-Go-Round (The Roman Citadel) – For all the fun of the fairground.
- Petitbonum Camp (The Roman Citadel) – Adventure playground.
- Gaul Huts (Asterix Village) – Run in and out of the world of Asterix.
- The Asterix Run (Asterix Village) – A boat trip through invaded France.
- The Little Train (Asterix Village) – For tiny tots.

- The Serpentine (Asterix Village) – Little big dipper.
- The Dolphinarium (The Great Lake) – Dolphin and sealion show.
- Les Petits Drakkars (The Great Lake) – Boats for little Vikings.
- The Little Swingchairs (The Great Lake) – For high fliers.
- Workshops (Rue de Paris) – Watch the craftsmen at work.
- The Little Carousel (Rue de Paris) – Wooden horses for little knights.
- Animal Studio (Rue de Paris) – Chance to be made-up into a superstar dog or cat.
- The Baby Bumper Chariots (Gergovie Square) – For baby Ben Hurs.
- The Trans-Arverne (Gergovie Square) – Tame roller-coaster for all the family.

Attractions for Thrill-Seekers
- Menhir Express – New water ride guaranteed to get you soaked!
- Goudurix (The Great Lake) – Stomach-churning roller-coaster.
- The Roman Galley (The Great Lake) –For those who like their stomach in their mouth.
- Big Splash (La Place de Gergovie) – A guaranteed soaking!

Attractions for History Buffs
- Rue de Paris (Rue de Paris) – This whole section traces ten centuries of French history.

Attractions not to be Missed
- The Gladiators' Arena (The Roman Citadel) – Entertaining warm-up for the Olympic Games.

- Down the Styx River (The Roman Citadel) – Fun water ride for all the family.
- Gaul Huts (Asterix Village) – Houses for Asterix and his friends.
- The Goudurix (The Great Lake) – Upside down view of the lake.
- Mediaeval Square (Rue de Paris) – Brilliant jugglers and acrobats.
- Dances from the Belle Epoque (Rue de Paris) – Flavour of Paris during that time.
- The Big Splash (Gergovie Square) – Chance to cool down on a hot summer's day.

Further Information
Bookings in UK, Tel: 0242 236 169.
150F adult (105F children 3–11 years old; free for children under three). Look out for special packages in 1995 in celebration of the twenty-fifth anniversary of Asterix in Britain.
Open from April to October.
Parc Asterix, Plailly (Tel: 44 62 32 10).

EXCURSION FIVE
PARC DE LOISIRS DE TORCY

Distance from Disneyland Paris:
8 km.

Directions from Disneyland Paris:
A4 west towards Paris then exit A104 towards Torcy and follow signs to Parc de Loisirs.

Why go to Parc de Loisirs?
- For a day on the beach.
- For a picnic.

● To do some sports.

Description
Parc de Loisirs is a 25-hectare lake with a wide range of sporting facilities including catamaran sailing, windsurfing, pony riding, canoeing, pedalos, mini golf and a sandy beach with marked-out swimming area. You have to pay to drive in, so it is worth taking a picnic and spending an afternoon or whole day there.

Further Information
Parc de Loisirs de Torcy, Marne-la-Vallée (Tel: 64 80 58 75).

EXCURSION SIX
PARIS

Distance from Disneyland Paris:
32 km.

Directions from Disneyland Paris:
A4 into Paris via Porte de Bercy. As parking is a problem in the centre of the city, it is easier to take the RER train direct from Disneyland Paris into the centre of Paris.

Why go to Paris?
● To see one of the most beautiful cities in the world.
● For sightseeing, museums, art and culture.
● To shop until you drop.
● For a romantic day out.

Description

Disneyland Paris is only half an hour by car or train from Paris, so, if you have a day to spare, it is certainly worth touring this beautiful city. My personal advice is to leave your car at Disneyland Paris and take the train, as otherwise you could spend the whole day trying to find somewhere to park. The centre of Paris, where you will find most of the following attractions, is fairly compact, so you should be able to tour it all by foot or by using their highly efficient metro system.

There is so much to see and do in the French capital that it it is hard to do it justice in one small section of a book. I have tried to group together different types of activities, so that you can easily plan your own itinerary before you go. Don't try to cram too much in a day or you will end up exhausted – the art treasures of the Louvre, for example, could easily be a whole-day excursion! When planning your day, try to choose attractions that are in a similar area, or are at least within walking distance. Travelling on foot is actually the best way to get the flavour of this wonderful city, so put your most comfortable shoes on and have a good day!

Shopaholics

If your trip to Disneyland Paris hasn't financially stripped you bare, Paris is one of the best cities in the world to shop and, even if money is tight, it can be almost as much fun browsing and window shopping.

Haute Couture: If you are looking for the top of French designer fashion, go to Avenue Montaigne and Faubourg St-Honoré. In Avenue Montaigne

(Champs-Elysées metro), you will find shops such as Karl Lagerfeld, Nina Ricci, Christian Dior, Louis Vuitton, Valentino and Cartier. In Faubourg St-Honoré (Madeléine metro) you will find Yves Saint Laurent, Lanvin, Hermès, Gucci, Chloë and Lacroix (for really outrageous and outrageously expensive outfits!).

Department Stores: For beautiful lingerie, designer clothes and fashion shows, go to Galeries Lafayette, 40 bvd Haussman (Chaussée d'Antin is the nearest metro). If you need a break from shopping, there is a fantastic view from the rooftop café at the art nouveau department store, La Samaritaine, 19 Rue de la Monnaie (Pont-Neuf metro). Perfume lovers will be in heaven in the huge perfume department at Printemps, 64 boulevard Haussmann (Havre-Caumartin metro) which also boasts a wide selection of top designer fashion.

Forum des Halles, *Rue Rambuteau* (Les Halles metro): This is the Parisian equivalent of Covent Garden, a glass, four-storey modern shopping centre, built on the old site of a wholesale fruit and vegetable market. Inside this subterranean shopping centre, you will find over 180 boutiques, mainly selling clothes. There is also a cinema, a swimming-pool and a museum.

Markets: You could spend a very enjoyable day indeed just wandering the Parisian markets. My personal favourite is the giant flea-market Marché aux Puces St Ouen (Porte de Clignancourt metro) which has over 3,000 stalls, divided between five separate markets on adjoining streets.

The Latin Quarter: This is a popular area for students and young Parisians. In Boulevard St-Michel (St Michel metro) you will find artsy clothing, bookshops and record stores. Also in this area is the picturesque open-air market La Mouffe (Monge metro) located in the bottom half of the medieval street, Rue Mouffetard.

St-Germain-des-Près (St-Germain-des-Près metro): This small, lively area on the left bank, near the Latin Quarter is a fashionable place to shop. Here you will find smart little art galleries, antique shops, bookshops and trendy clothes boutiques. It is a wonderful area just to stroll around window shopping or for just sitting in the street cafés (see page 262).

Four Famous Landmarks

The Eiffel Tower, Quai Branly (Trocadéro metro): Built in 1889 for the World Fair, on the centenary of the Revolution, this 300-metre iron structure has become one of the main symbols of Paris. From the top, the views are spectacular – covering over 40 miles on a good day. As this is one of the most popular tourist attractions in Paris (four million visitors go up to the top each year), be prepared to queue.

Arc de Triomphe, Place Charles de Gaulle (Etoile metro): Another Parisian symbol that we all know so well. It was commissioned in 1806 by Napoleon I in honour of the Grand Army, although he never actually saw it completed. Underneath the monument is the Tomb of the Unknown Soldier, erected in commemoration of all those who died in the First World War. You can pay to go up to the platform at the top which gives a brilliant view of the 12 avenues spanning out around it.

Nôtre Dame, Place du Parvis (Cité metro): This stunningly beautiful gothic cathedral has been rebuilt several times since its foundations were laid in 1163 by Pope Alexander III. It suffered greatly in the Revolution, when it was used as a wine store, but survived the Nazi occupation by having all its beautiful stained-glass windows carefully removed for safekeeping. The original rose windows are absolutely spectacular.

Sacré Coeur, 35 Rue Chevalie de la Barre (Abbesses metro): The foundations of this famous white-domed church were laid in 1870. You can either take a lift or walk up to the top for another breathtaking view of the city.

Culture Vultures

The selection and quality of museums in Paris is outstanding. State-owned museums such as the Louvre are closed on either Mondays or Tuesdays and offer free admission on Wednesdays or Sundays. The best time to tour the museums is a weekday lunchtime (apart from Wednesday if there is free admission) as they are usually less crowded then. You can check the opening hours of museums in *Pariscope*, a weekly listings magazine.

Following is a selection of some of the most interesting museums in Paris. If you plan to spend the whole day touring museums you can buy a Museums and Monuments card for 55F which gives you entry to 63 musuems and monuments in Paris and enables you to jump the queues. Cards are available from Association Inter-Musées, 25 Rue du Renard, 75004, Paris (Tel: 44 78 45 81).

George Pompidou National Art and Culture Centre, Rue Rambuteau and Rue St-Merri (Rambuteau or Hôtel-de-Ville metros). Closed on Tuesdays.

Also known as the Beaubourg, the Pompidou Centre is the sort of place you instantly either love or hate. Its famous inside-out architecture features a futuristic escalator (expect to queue) up the outside of the building. From the cafeteria at the top, there is a superb view of the city, while on the fourth floor, you will find the National Museum of Modern Art which exhibits art from 1905 to 1965, including works by Picasso, Henri Rousseau, Dali, Matisse, Mondrian, Kandinsky and Magritte. On the third floor, you will find contemporary paintings (1965 onwards) – these are varied two or three times a year to give younger artists a chance of becoming better known.

This lively art centre also houses a cinema, an industrial design area and a photographic gallery. Outside on the cobbled terrace, there is always a colourful selection of jugglers, fire-eaters, acrobats and street performers, as well as a children's workshop (see page 266).

Science Museum (La Cité des Sciences et de l'Industrie) Parc de la Villette, 30 Ave Corentin-Cariou (Porte de la Villette metro). Closed on Mondays.

Located in this 55-hectare park, the Science

Museum is a fascinating place for both adults and children. Built in 1986, the futuristic interior of the museum is quite spectacular and is designed like a scientific playground in which you explore and participate, rather than just view exhibits. Experience weightlessness on a trip into space, watch a film inside a hemispherical cinema housed in the spectacular space-age 'Geode' theatre, or play with some of the many video games and gadgets. There is so much to experience in this museum that you could easily spend at least half a day there.

English brochures and cassettes are available. There is also an Inventorium which runs discovery sessions for children (see Child's Play, page 264).

Musée du Louvre, Rue de Rivoli (Palais Royal or Louvre metro). Closed on Tuesdays.

The foundations of this building were first laid in 1200 by Philip Augustus and the palace was first opened to the public in 1793 – four years after the Revolution. It now houses hundreds of thousands of works of art, including such world-famous masterpieces as the *Mona Lisa* and *Venus de Milo*. Due to the size of the musuem, you could easily spend several days here. If you only have a few hours, it is best to buy an English guidebook so that you can decide which sections are of most interest to you. The collections include Egyptian antiquities, Oriental antiquities, Greek and Roman antiquities, objets d'art and an enormous collection of paintings from all the European schools (English, Italian, Flemish, Dutch, German and Spanish) – but predominantly French.

The main entrance to the musuem is in the controversial glass pyramid, designed by Pei and erected in the centre of the Cour Napoleon in 1988.

Musée d'Orsay, 1 Rue de Bellechasse (Solferino metro). Closed on Mondays.

Closed on Tuesdays. Collections here span from the late 1840s to 1914 and aim to cover the gap between what you will find at the Louvre and at the Pompidou Centre. Here you will find the main collection of Impressionist art in Paris as well as a superb display of art nouveau.

Musée Picasso, Hotel Sale, 5 Rue de Thorigny (St Paul metro). Closed on Tuesdays.

This museum is housed in one of the finest former private residences of the Marais district and comprises the largest single collection of Picasso's paintings, sculptures and personal memorabilia.

Musée de l'Orangerie, Place de la Concorde (Concorde metro). Closed on Tuesdays. The *Water-Lilies* galleries are sometimes closed in the lunch hour.

Claude Monet enthusiasts will love this small, airy museum which exhibits Monet's *Water-Lilies*, eight huge compositions painted at Giverny between 1915 and the artist's death. Upstairs the Jean Walker and Paul Guillaume collection includes work by Sisley, Cezanne, Renoir, Picasso, Matisse, Rousseau and Modigliani.

Coach Tours

If you are unlucky enough to choose a rainy day in

Paris, one of the best ways to sightsee and stay dry is to go on an organised coach tour. This is also a good way to get a feel for how the city is laid out – most tours last about two hours and cover all the major sites. English commentaries (usually pre-recorded) are available.

Try Paris Vision, offering tours of Paris, as well as excursions to places reviewed in this chapter, such as Fontainebleau and Barbizon; Chantilly; and Vaux-le-Vicomte and Fontainebleau. Coaches depart from 214 Rue de Rivoli (Tel: 42 60 31 25) or Cityrama, departing from the Cityrama bus-stop, 4 Place des Pyramides (Tel: 44 55 61 00).

River Rats

One of the most romantic and rewarding ways to see Paris is by boat. This is a good way of getting your bearings and discovering where the famous landmarks are. It is also fun for children. English-speaking commentaries are available. Lunch, tea and candlelit dinner cruises are on offer.

Les Vedettes du Pont Neuf (Tel: 46 33 98 38) Pont Neuf metro.

A one-hour boat trip from Nôtre Dame to the Eiffel Tower and back. An English-speaking commentary is available and boats leave from behind the equestrian statue in the middle of the Pont Neuf bridge. Children can go on this trip unaccompanied – this is left to the parents' discretion.

Bâteaux-Mouches Pont de l'Alma (Tel: 42 25 96 10) Alma-Marceau metro.

Strollers and Café Lizards

One of the best ways to get the real flavour of Paris is to spend a couple of hours just strolling around the streets. Following are some of the most interesting areas for exploring on foot.

The most pleasant way to rest your feet afterwards is to sit and relax in a café, a perfect place for people-watching. Be warned, however, about the Parisian scale of charges. Drinks are often priced according to where you consume them, the cheapest is at the counter, the most expensive is sitting on the terrace (prime spot for people-watching). Nearly all Parisian cafés serve coffee, alcohol, sandwiches and other snacks, so, once you have a table, you can happily sit there for an hour or two and just watch the Parisian world walk by.

Montmartre (Anvers metro)

Montmartre automatically conjures up images of dance shows and the cancan captured on canvas by Toulouse Lautrec, and it is still a very popular place with painters, poets, writers, musicians and actors. Today the main tourist attraction at Montmartre is the Sacré Coeur (see page 257), although it is worth visiting this hilly village just to wander around the picturesque streets and soak in the bohemian atmosphere.

Don't linger too long at the over-commercialised Place du Tertre where dozens of artists clamour to paint your portrait and overpriced restaurants cash in on the popularity of the square. It is much more interesting to explore the quieter backstreets where you will find peaceful little squares, cobbled alleyways and village houses which actually have front gardens (very unusual for Paris!). Place Émile-Goudeau has always been a favourite spot with artists, including Picasso and Matisse, and this is a good place to sit in a café and watch the arty world go by.

Not far from Montmartre, at the bottom of the hill, you will find Pigalle (Pigalle metro), the nightlife district of Paris, full of neon lights and strip shows. The most famous venue is the Moulin Rouge on the Boulevard de Clichy.

St-Germain-des-Près (St-Germain-des-Près metro)

Located on the left bank, this tiny little area is always fashionable and is lively both day and night. After strolling around looking at the little galleries and arty shops (see above), take a seat on the terrace at Les Deux Magots, 6 Place Saint-Germain-des-Près, or Café de Flore, 172 Boulevard Saint-Germain. Just round the corner from each other, both of these are famous literary cafés which writers such as Gide, Sartre and Hemingway used to frequent.

Montparnasse (Vavin metro)

This is still the heart of Parisian café society with famous places such as La Coupole (102 Boulevard Montparnasse), a stylish art-deco restaurant which still holds tea dances; the traditional Le Select (99 Boulevard Montparnasse) and La Rotonde (105 Boulevard Montparnasse) where the names of famous people who used to go there, including Lenin and Trotsky, are immortally inscribed on the menu.

The Champs-Elysées (Charles de Gaulle Etoile
metro for the Arc de Triomphe end)
A stroll along the Champs-Elysées is almost a
must on a first-time visit to Paris. Sadly, this wide
avenue has lost its former grandeur and is now
packed with fast-food restaurants and neon signs.
There is, however, so much history attached to
the Champs-Elysées that it will always be a great
landmark of the city. Marie-Antoinette and Louis
XVI were just a couple of the people executed
here in the Revolution. And Hitler marched his
army down this long avenue in 1940, only for the
French to celebrate victory there a few years
later.

A walk down the Champs-Elysées will enable
you to see many major sights including the Arc de
Triomphe, the Eiffel Tower and the Place de la
Concorde. You can then continue through the
Jardin des Tuileries where you will find the
Orangerie Museum, before finally reaching the
Louvre.

Child's Play

Paris is not usually associated with being a place
for children, but there is actually plenty for
them to do and see. Following are some suggestions.

The Parisian Circus (Cirque de Paris) Avenue
de la Commune-de-Paris, Nanterre (RER
Nanterre Ville)
Located on the outskirts west of Paris, what
makes this circus particularly unusual and

appealing to children is that they can spend a day here actually learning the skills of the circus. They can be made up like a clown, learn how to juggle or walk a tightrope. A day's ticket includes participation workshops, lunch with the circus artists, and a show in the afternoon. Adults are also welcome.

Children's Playground (Jardin des Enfants)
105 Rue Rambuteau (Les Halles metro)

If your children are nagging you because they are bored of the Pompidou Centre or shopping at Les Halles, pacify them by taking them to this supervised open-air adventure playground for 7–11 year olds. Group activities are organised or children can play on their own. Parents are only allowed in on Saturdays when they can bring younger children.

Jardin d'Acclimatation Bois de Boulogne
(Porte Maillot metro)

If you feel like spending an afternoon relaxing in the fresh air, the Bois de Boulogne is the perfect spot for families. There are all sorts of sports facilities in the park including a free roller-skating rink, a jogging track and bicycles for rent. The Jardin d'Acclimatation is a special pleasure park for children. The most enjoyable way to get there is chugging through the woods aboard the 'pleasure train' which departs from near the Porte Maillot metro entrance. Inside the turnstiles, you will find a small zoo, a puppet theatre, a playground for the under-12s, a hall of mirrors, dodgem cars, a mini-motorcycle course, donkey rides and boat trips down the 'enchanted river'.

Science and Technology Museum (Cité des Sciences et de l'Industrie) Parc de la Villette, 30 Ave Corentin-Cariou (Porte de la Villette metro)

This museum is lots of fun for all the family (see Culture Vultures above). The Inventorium (L'Inventorium) is a special section for children which runs 90-minute discovery sessions in which children can learn about science through play. Adults are only allowed in when accompanied by children!

The Waxworks (Musée Grevin) 10 Boulevard Montmartre (Rue Montmartre metro)

Learn some of the grim details of the French Revolution and see lifelike models of pop stars, film stars and politicians.

Children's Workshop (Atelier des Enfants) Centre Georges Pompidou (Châtelet or Les Halles metro)

If you want to tour the Pompidou Centre you can leave children over five on a Wednesday or Saturday here to participate in supervised activities, like games, painting and sculpture. Children who do not speak any French may feel a little lost here, though.

The Cousteau Oceanic Park (Parc Océanique Cousteau), Forum des Halles (Châtelet or Les Halles metro)

Explore the depths of the ocean through audio-visual experience.

Zoo de Vincennes (53 Avenue de Saint Maurice. Porte Dorée metro)

Instead of being in cages, most of the animals here

are separated from the public by high walls and moats. There is also a miniature train that tours around the zoo and park. Afterwards you can go for a boat trip on the lake.

The Sewers of Paris (Les Egouts de Paris)
Place de la Résistance (Alma Marceau metro)
If your children are into bad smells and squalor, they may find an organised tour of the Parisian sewers fascinating!

Further Information
Central Tourist Information Office 127 Avenue des Champs-Elysées (Tel: 49 52 53 54) Etoile or George V metro
The place to pick up brochures, maps and tourist information about Paris.

EXCURSION SEVEN
VAUX-LE-VICOMTE

Distance from Disneyland Paris:
44 km.

Directions from Disneyland Paris:
Drive west A4 towards Paris, exit Emerainville/ Melun (N104) and drive to Melun, then take N36 and follow signs to Vaux-le-Vicomte.

Why go to Vaux-le-Vicomte?
● To see the inspiration behind Versailles.
● A less touristy alternative to Versailles.
● As a combined excursion with Fontainebleau (see page 241).
● To tour the beautiful gardens.

Description

This fairytale château dates back to the seventeenth century when it was built for Nicolas Fouquet, Superintendent of the Treasury and one of the wealthiest men in France. He used three of France's most talented men to build Vaux-le-Vicomte – architect Louis le Vau, painter Charles le Brun and landscape gardener André le Nôtre.

In 1661, Fouquet hosted the most lavish party ever given at the château and invited the young king of the time, Louis XIV. Unfortunately, the splendour of the occasion evoked the king's jealousy and a few weeks later he had Fouquet arrested and charged with swindling the treasury funds.

With Fouquet behind bars, Louis XIV now set about building an even grander château and commissioned le Vau, le Brun and le Nôtre to set to work on Versailles.

Vaux-le-Vicomte was sold by Fouquet's widow before it was finished and today you can see the unfinished work of le Brun in the Grand Salon. The estate was bought in 1875 by the Sommier family who saved and restored this magnificent château and gardens.

A tour around the interior of the château is fascinating, and the grounds with their sculpted hedges, pools and fountains are truly stunning. There are also fountain displays on the second and last Saturday afternoon of every month.

Further Information

Vaux-le-Vicomte, 77950 Maincy (Tel: 64 37 11 31)
Closed during December and January.

CHAPTER FOURTEEN

THE UNOFFICIAL DISNEY QUIZ

Below are a selection of questions to test you and your family's knowledge of the wonderful world of Disney.

1. Which was the first Walt Disney sound cartoon?
2. What is the man-cub called in *The Jungle Book*?
3. Where and when did Disneyland open?
4. Which was the first full-length animated feature film?
5. What was the original name intended for the famous Disney mouse?
6. Who taught Dumbo to fly?
7. What is the name of Mickey's girlfriend?
8. What are the names of Donald Duck's nephews?
9. What character starred as the Sorcerer's Apprentice in *Fantasia*?
10. What sort of animal is Uncle Scrooge?
11. What colour of nose does Chip have?
12. What colour of nose does Dale have?
13. What is Walt Disney's middle name?
14. When was Walt Disney born?
15. For what did Disney win his first Academy Award?
16. What year did Walt Disney die?
17. When did the EPCOT centre open at the Walt Disney World Resort?

18. When did Tokyo Disneyland open?
19. When did Disney-MGM Studios open at the Walt Disney World Resort?
20. Who is Ariel's crabby friend?
21. In which cartoon do Figaro and Cleo feature?
22. Who is in charge of the *Nautilus*?
23. Who was born on 18 November 1928?
24. In which film did the calypso song 'Under the Sea' feature?
25. Complete the question which the wicked queen asked of her mirror:
    'Magic mirror on the wall . . .'
26. From the basement of which New York landmark did the International Rescue Aid Society in *The Rescuers* operate?
27. In which year was *Bedknobs and Broomsticks* released?
28. Who gets wet in *An April Shower*?
29. Mickey Mouse co-starred with which Disney favourite in no less than 26 cartoons between 1935 and 1942?
30. What type of accent does Disney's Scrooge have?
31. What do the Dwarfs sing on their way home from work?
32. Who played the part of Pinocchio's conscience?
33. Who bobbed along at the bottom of the beautiful briny sea?
34. Which classical composition inspired the vision of Mount Olympus in *Fantasia*?
35. Can you name all Seven Dwarfs?
36. Who plays Cratchite in Mickey's *Christmas Carol*?
37. Who gave Hitler the Bronx cheer in Disney's wartime propaganda feature *Der Fuehrer Face*?
38. From which song and which film do the following lyrics come:
    'I've seen a peanut stand, I've seen a rubber band . . .'?
39. Which film was based on the Joel Chandler Harris *Uncle Remus* stories, starring Br'er Fox?
40. What did the queen order the huntsman to do to Snow White?

41. Who was the leader of the pack of wolves in *The Jungle Book*?

42. In which film did the fierce cat Lucifer terrify the house mice?

43. With what does the queen poison Snow White?

44. Whose play provided the inspiration for the 1951 Disney movie *Peter Pan*?

45. Which animated feature used CinemaScope (using a wider than usual screen) for the first time?

46. How do Perdita and Pongo broadcast their news in *101 Dalmatians*?

47. Which Disney feature had a titanic dragon fight for a climax?

48. What was the name of the brother of albatross Orville, who appeared in the movie *The Rescuers Down Under*?

49. Who tells the dwarfs that Snow White has been poisoned?

50. Which band's lead singer was cast as the bear Baloo in *The Jungle Book*?

51. Which favourite tale of the French Court in the mid-seventeenth century became a Disney feature in the 1990s?

52. What was the last animated feature in which Walt Disney took part?

53. How many Oscars has Walt Disney won?

54. From which feature is this line taken:
    'Whoso pulleth out this sword . . . is rightwise King of England'?

55. How did the Prince awaken Snow White?

56. What was the name of the shy janitor who helped Bianca in *The Rescuers*?

57. Which hero of classic English folklore portrayed in a classic Disney feature has also been played by Errol Flynn and Kevin Costner?

58. Who started his career with Disney before leaving to become director of *Beetlejuice*, *Batman* and *Edward Scissorhands*?

59. On which fictional English character was the hero of the *The Great Mouse Detective* based?

60. What did Snow White find upstairs in the dwarfs' cottage?

61. Pop stars Bette Midler, Billy Joel and Cheech Marin supplied the voices for which Disney feature based on a Charles Dickens novel?

62. How do the Dalmatian puppies disguise themselves in order to escape?

63. In which country was the sequel to *The Rescuers* based?

64. Where in Disneyland Paris will you find 999 grisly ghouls?

65. How does the queen disguise herself when she comes to poison Snow White?

66. Who was the purringly evil tiger in *The Jungle Book*?

67. In which Disney film was the Busby Berkeley production number 'Be Our Guest' featured?

68. According to Charles Perrault's seventeenth-century tale, what is the name of the Sleeping Beauty?

69. How many puppies do Perdita and Pongo have?

70. Who made his debut in the 1934 Silly Symphony, *The Wise Little Hen*?

71. Which cartoon features 'When You Wish Upon A Star'?

72. What is the name of Baloo's sure-fire musical hit in *The Jungle Book*?

73. Which of Mickey's bashful pals is often heard to exclaim 'Gawrsh!'?

74. The eerie Skull Rock overshadows which famous Disneyland Paris attraction?

75. Fifi the Peke and Dinah the Dachshund were wooed by which of Mickey's pals?

76. Who had a sister named Dumbella?

77. Who were the two pesky chipmunks who plagued Donald Duck and who later starred in their own series?

78. Who was Anita's horrible friend in *101 Dalmatians*?

79. What is the name of the main thoroughfare through Disneyland Paris?

80. How many steam trains leave Main Street Station in Disneyland Paris for a grand tour?

81. Veteran American comedian Bob Newhart supplied the lead voices for the same character in which two Disney features?

82. Where in Disneyland Paris can you be entertained by cancan dancers?

83. Which Disneyland Paris hotel boasts an ice-rink in winter?

84. Who lived with Roger Radcliff before he got married?

85. The *How to . . .* series of cartoon shorts, which ran until the mid-1950s, were the star vehicle for whom?

86. Who wrote the beautiful Sleeping Beauty ballet music which sets the scene inside Disneyland Paris's Château de la Belle au Bois Dormant?

87. Who was reduced to a mantel clock by the sorceress's spell in *Beauty and the Beast*?

88. What fearsome fire-breathing beast lurks in the dungeon of Sleeping Beauty's Castle?

89. Where can you stay Wild West style in Disneyland Paris?

90. What was the name of Anita's Dalmatian?

91. On which day in 1992 did Disneyland Paris open?

92. What does Cruella de Vil want the Dalmatian puppies for?

93. What does Snow White give each dwarf before they go to work?

94. 'Who's Afraid Of The Big Bad Wolf?' was the rallying cry of the stars of which 1933 Disney cartoon?

95. How many Dalmatian puppies were stolen?

96. Who wrote the original tale of *The Little Mermaid*?

97. Which animal family originally adopts the man-cub in *The Jungle Book*?

98. What was the name of the bloodhound in the 1930 Mickey Mouse cartoon, *The Chain Gang*, who became a Disney regular?

99. Which veteran star of horror films supplied the voice for the archvillain Ratigan in *The Great Mouse Detective*?

100. Who taught Mowgli how to survive the jungle?

101. Which film featured the song 'A Whole New World', which won two Academy Awards?

102. What is the name of the wicked uncle in *The Lion King*?

Answers

1. *Steamboat Willie.*
2. Mowgli.
3. 1955 at Anaheim, California.
4. *Snow White*, released in 1937.
5. Mortimer. Mickey was chosen to please Walt Disney's wife.
6. Timothy the mouse.
7. Minnie.
8. Huey, Louie and Dewey.
9. Mickey Mouse.
10. A duck.
11. Black.
12. Red.
13. Elias.
14. 5 December 1901.
15. *Flowers and Trees*, 1932.
16. 15 December 1966.
17. 1982.
18. 1983.
19. 1989.
20. Sebastian.
21. Pinocchio.
22. Captain Nemo.
23. Mickey Mouse.
24. *The Little Mermaid.*
25. 'Who's the fairest of them all?'
26. The United Nations Building.
27. 1971.
28. Bambi.
29. Donald Duck.
30. Scottish.
31. 'Heigh-ho! Heigh-ho! It's home from work we go!'
32. Jiminy Cricket.
33. Angela Lansbury and David Tomlinson (*Bedknobs and Broomsticks*).
34. Beethoven's Sixth Symphony.
35. Doc, Grumpy, Happy, Bashful, Sleepy, Sneezy and Dopey.
36. Mickey Mouse.
37. Donald Duck.
38. 'When I see an Elephant Fly.' Dumbo.
39. *Song of the South.*
40. To kill her.
41. Akela.
42. *Cinderella.*
43. A poisoned red apple.
44. James M. Barrie.
45. *The Lady and the Tramp.*
46. The twilight bark.
47. *Sleeping Beauty.*
48. Wilbur.
49. The animals.
50. Phil Harris.
51. *Beauty and the Beast.*
52. *The Jungle Book.*
53. Twenty.
54. *The Sword and the Stone.*
55. With a kiss.
56. Bernard.
57. Robin Hood.
58. Tim Burton.
59. Sherlock Holmes.
60. Seven unmade beds.
61. *Oliver and Company.*

62. They roll in soot so they look like black Labradors.
63. Australia.
64. Phantom Manor.
65. As an old woman.
66. Shere Khan.
67. *Beauty and the Beast*.
68. Princess Aurora.
69. Fifteen.
70. Donald Duck.
71. Pinocchio.
72. 'The Bare Necessities'.
73. Goofy.
74. Pirates of the Caribbean.
75. Pluto.
76. Donald Duck.
77. Chip an' Dale.
78. Cruella de Vil.
79. Main Street, USA.
80. Three.
81. *The Rescuers* and *The Rescuers Down Under*.
82. The Lucky Nugget Saloon in Frontierland.
83. Hotel New York.
84. Pongo.
85. Goofy.
86. Tchaikovsky.
87. Cogsworth.
88. A dragon.
89. Hotel Cheyenne.
90. Perdita.
91. 12 April.
92. To make fur coats out of their beautiful skins.
93. A kiss.
94. *The Three Little Pigs*.
95. Ninety-nine.
96. Hans Christian Andersen.
97. The wolves.
98. Pluto.
99. Vincent Price.
100. Baloo.
101. Aladdin.
102. Scar.

CHAPTER FIFTEEN

WHERE TO FIND YOUR FAVOURITE DISNEY CHARACTERS

From the moment you walk through the gates, you will have plenty of opportunity to meet your favourite Disney characters. They will happily shake your hand and pose for photos with you and your children.

Young children will particularly enjoy the Disney Parade and the Main Street Electrical Parade where they can see so many of their favourite characters – like Mickey Mouse, Baloo, Cinderella, Goofy (Dingo, in French), Donald Duck, Pluto, Roger Rabbit and Chip and Dale (Tic et Tac, in French). Other good places to meet the Disney characters include the special character breakfast and the C'est Magique show on Fantasy Festival Stage.

In this chapter, we tell you which rides and attractions feature certain characters. We have included their 'date of birth' – this refers to when the Disney characters originated. However, many of them are actually a lot older as they have been derived from classic stories and plays.

Name: **ALADDIN**
In French: Aladdin
Date of birth: 1993, in the Disney animated feature *Aladdin*.
Where to find Aladdin in Disneyland Paris: Le Passage Enchanté d'Aladdin.
Characteristics: Street-smart peasant who has a monkey called Abu as his best friend.

Name: **ALICE**
In French: Alice
Date of birth: 1951, in the Disney cartoon *Alice in Wonderland*, based on Lewis Carroll's story.
Where to find Alice in Disneyland Paris: Alice's Curious Labyrinth (Fantasyland).
Characteristics: Pretty little blonde girl, famous for her Alice band.

Name: **BASHFUL**
In French: Timide
Date of birth: Christmas 1937, in the film *Snow White and the Seven Dwarfs*.
Where to find Bashful in Disneyland Paris: Snow White and the Seven Dwarfs (Fantasyland).
Characteristics: Bashful expression, bulbous nose, broad cheeks and white beard. Wears a long cap.

Name: **CAPTAIN HOOK**
In French: Capitaine Crochet
Date of birth: 1953, in the film *Peter Pan*, based on J.M. Barrie's play.
Where to find Captain Hook in Disneyland Paris: Peter Pan's Flight (Fantasyland).
Characteristic: A metal hook for his left hand which was eaten by a crocodile.

277

Name: **CHESHIRE CAT**
In French: Chester
Date of birth: 1951, in the film *Alice in Wonderland.*
Where to find the Cheshire Cat in Disneyland Paris: Alice's Curious Labyrinth.
Characteristic: Huge, beaming smile.

Name: **CLEO**
In French: Cleo
Date of birth: 1940, in the film *Pinocchio,* based on the tale by Carlo Collodi.
Where to find Cleo in Disneyland Paris: Pinocchio's Adventures (Fantasyland).
Characteristics: A goldfish.

Name: **DOC**
In French: Prof
Date of birth: Christmas 1937, in the film *Snow White and the Seven Dwarfs.*
Where to find Doc in Disneyland Paris: Snow White and the Seven Dwarfs (Fantasyland).
Characteristics: Pompous, self-appointed leader of the seven dwarfs. Broad cheeks, bulbous nose, white beard and wears a long cap.

Name: **DOPEY**
In French: Simplet
Date of birth: Christmas 1937, in the film *Snow White and the Seven Dwarfs.*
Where to find Dopey in Disneyland Paris: Snow White and the Seven Dwarfs (Fantasyland).
Characteristics: Human with the mannerisms and intellect of a dog. Shows off with a slap-happy dance. Broad cheeks, bulbous nose and wears a long cap. Doesn't speak.

Name: **DUMBO**
In French: Dumbo
Date of birth: 1941, in the cartoon *Dumbo.*
Where to find Dumbo in Disneyland Paris: Dumbo the Flying Elephant (Fantasyland).
Characteristics: Baby elephant who learns to fly.

Name: **FIGARO**
In French: Figaro
Date of birth: 1940, in the film *Pinocchio.*
Where to find Figaro in Disneyland Paris: Pinocchio's Adventures.
Characteristics: Geppetto's cat.

Name: **GEPPETTO**
In French: Geppetto
Date of birth: 1940, in the film *Pinocchio.*
Where to find Geppetto in Disneyland Paris: Pinocchio's Adventures (Fantasyland).
Characteristics: Old man, woodcarver and father of Pinocchio.

Name: **GRUMPY**
In French: Grincheaux
Date of birth: Christmas 1937, in the film *Snow White and the Seven Dwarfs.*
Where to find Grumpy in Disneyland Paris: Snow White and the Seven Dwarfs (Fantasyland).
Characteristics: Perpetual scowl, broad cheeks, bulbous nose, white beard and long cap.

Name: **HAPPY**
In French: Joyeux
Date of birth: Christmas 1937, in the film *Snow White and the Seven Dwarfs.*

Where to find Happy in Disneyland Paris: Snow White and the Seven Dwarfs (Fantasyland).
Characteristics: Always smiling. Broad cheeks, bulbous nose, white beard and long cap.

Name: **JIMINY CRICKET**
In French: Jiminy Criquet
Date of birth: 1940, in the film *Pinocchio.*
Where to find Jiminy Cricket in Disneyland Paris: Pinocchio's Adventures (Fantasyland).
Characteristics: Little cricket who wears a top hat, white gloves and carries an umbrella. Acts as Pinocchio's conscience.

Name: **MAD HATTER**
In French: Le Chapelier Fou
Date of birth: 1951, in the film *Alice in Wonderland.*
Where to find the Mad Hatter in Disneyland Paris: Mad Hatter's Teacups (Fantasyland).
Characteristics: Eccentric character who celebrates 'unbirthdays' and loves holding tea parties.

Name: **MONSTRO THE WHALE**
In French: Monstro la Baleine
Date of birth: 1940, in the film, *Pinocchio.*
Where to find Monstro the Whale in Disneyland Paris: Pinocchio's Adventures (Fantasyland).
Characteristics: Huge whale who swallows Pinocchio.

Name: **PETER PAN**
In French: Peter Pan
Date of birth: 1953, in the film *Peter Pan*, based on J.M. Barrie's play.

Where to find Peter Pan in Disneyland Paris: Peter Pan's Flight (Fantasyland).
Characteristics: Little boy in Robin Hood-type costume who can fly and who refuses to grow up.

Name: **PINOCCHIO**
In French: Pinocchio
Date of birth: 1940, in the film *Pinnochio.*
Where to find Pinocchio in Disneyland Paris: Pinocchio's Adventures (Fantasyland).
Characteristics: Little puppet boy who comes to life and whose nose grows when he tells a fib.

Name: **SLEEPY**
In French: Dormeur
Date of birth: Christmas 1937, in the film *Snow White and the Seven Dwarfs.*
Where to find Sleepy in Disneyland Paris: Snow White and the Seven Dwarfs (Fantasyland).
Characteristics: Droopy-eyed dwarf with broad cheeks, bulbous nose, white beard and long cap.

Name: **SNEEZY**
In French: Atchoum
Date of birth: Christmas 1937, in the film *Snow White and the Seven Dwarfs.*
Where to find Sneezy in Disneyland Paris: Snow White and the Seven Dwarfs (Fantasyland).
Characteristics: Broad cheeks, bulbous nose that is always twitching, white beard, and long cap.

Name: **SNOW WHITE**
In French: Blanche Neige
Date of birth: Christmas 1937, in *Snow White and the Seven Dwarfs.*

Where to find Snow White in Disneyland Paris:
Snow White and the Seven Dwarfs (Fantasyland).
Characteristics: Dark hair, fair skin, happy disposition.

Name: **TINKERBELL**
In French: Clochette
Date of birth: 1953, in the film *Peter Pan*, based on
J.M. Barrie's play.
Where to find Tinkerbell in Disneyland Paris: Peter
Pan's Flight (Fantasyland).
Characteristics: Cute little fairy who teaches Peter
how to fly.

Name: **WENDY**
In French: Wendy
Date of birth: 1953, in the film *Peter Pan*, based on
J.M. Barrie's play.
Where to find Wendy in Disneyland Paris: Peter
Pan's Flight (Fantasyland).
Characteristics: Girlfriend of Peter Pan who flies
to Never-Never-Land with him.

Name: **WICKED QUEEN**
In French: La Reine
Date of birth: Christmas 1937, in the film *Snow
White and the Seven Dwarfs.*
*Where to find the Wicked Queen in Disneyland
Paris:* Snow White and the Seven Dwarfs
(Fantasyland).
Characteristics: Furiously jealous of Snow White's
natural good looks, she disguises herself as an old
witch and tries to kill Snow White with a poisoned
apple.

Index